VEDIC ASTROLOGY
Simply Put

"The 12 Nagas, or Serpents of Time, looking at Jyotish, the Eye of Nature, as it glances at the planets in their cosmic motion."

To the owner of this horoscope, may the Sun God give auspiciousness,

the Moon excellent beauty, Mars wealth, Mercury intelligence and learning,

Jupiter an exceedingly long life, Venus kingdom, Saturn success, Rahu

abundant eminence, and Ketu fulfillment of desires.

— Hora Ratnam

ALSO BY WILLIAM R. LEVACY

Beneath a Vedic Sky: *A Beginner's Guide to the Astrology of Ancient India*

Beneath a Vedic Sun: *Discover Your Life Purpose with Vedic Astrology*

❦ ❦ ❦

HAY HOUSE TITLES OF RELATED INTEREST

Astrology Through a Psychic's Eyes, by Sylvia Browne

Born to Be Together: *Love, Relationships, Astrology, and the Soul,* by Terry Lamb

Colors & Numbers: *Your Personal Guide to Positive Vibrations in Daily Life,* by Louise L. Hay

The Complete Book of Numerology: *Discovering the Inner Self,* by David A. Phillips, Ph.D.

The Ultimate Astrologer, by Nicholas Campion

❦ ❦ ❦

All of the above are available at your local bookstore, or may be ordered by visiting:

Hay House USA: **www.hayhouse.com®**
Hay House Australia: **www.hayhouse.com.au**
Hay House UK: **www.hayhouse.co.uk**
Hay House South Africa: **orders@psdprom.co.za**
Hay House India: **www.hayhouseindia.co.in**

VEDIC ASTROLOGY
Simply Put

An Illustrated Guide
to the Astrology of Ancient India

William R. Levacy

HAY HOUSE, INC.
Carlsbad, California
London • Sydney • Johannesburg
Vancouver • Hong Kong • New Delhi

Published and distributed in the United States by: Hay House, Inc.: www.hayhouse.com • *Published and distributed in Australia by:* Hay House Australia Pty. Ltd.: www.hayhouse.com.au • *Published and distributed in the United Kingdom by:* Hay House UK, Ltd.: www.hayhouse.co.uk • *Published and distributed in the Republic of South Africa by:* Hay House SA (Pty), Ltd.: orders@psdprom.co.za • *Distributed in Canada by:* Raincoast: www.raincoast.com • *Published in India by:* Hay House Publications (India) Pvt. Ltd.: www.hayhouseindia.co.in

Editorial supervision: Jill Kramer • *Design:* Amy Gingery • *Interior illustrations:* Arumugan Manivel, S. Rajam (courtesy of *Hinduism Today*), Deepak Ganirwali, Sandeep Jain, Yupa Kiratiyannond, and Bangalore Sureshwara

Library of Congress Cataloging-in-Publication Data

Levacy, William R.
  Vedic astrology simply put : an illustrated guide to the astrology
of ancient India / William R. Levacy.
    p. cm.
  Includes bibliographical references.
  ISBN-13: 978-1-4019-0718-1 (hardcover)
  1. Hindu astrology.   I. Title.
BF1714.H5L52 2007
133.5'9445--dc22   2006021467

ISBN 13: 978-1-4019-0718-1

10 09 08 07   4 3 2 1
1st edition, April 2007

Printed in China

Contents

Ganesh writing the Vedas.

THE PURPOSE
OF THIS BOOK

Vedic astrology, or *Jyotish* (jyoh' tish), as it's called in India, is the Science or Knowledge of Time. Its purpose, over its several millennia of existence, has been to identify karma, or action, in terms of the past, present, and future. Vedic astrology is about understanding how to best perform in time. It's a behavior analysis and forecasting system, based on astronomical calculations, that helps us anticipate the benefits and challenges that lie ahead. Vedic astrology informs us of ways to modify our actions for the better. So while we might naturally have the will to take action, Vedic astrology prepares us for it in the best way.

The field of Vedic astrology has such a richness of tradition, myth, and philosophy. It offers wisdom principles that are both engaging and relevant to our modern times—yet it has a recorded history that dates back several thousand millennia and an oral tradition that some say precedes history itself. I have a love for Vedic philosophy and astrology that began specifically in 1970, in Eureka, California, with my initiation into meditation (it's interesting that *Eureka* means "I've found it!"). Building on that over the years, I wanted to create a small book on Vedic astrology that would contain colorful illustrations, diagrams, and informative tables to help simplify the study of this beautiful, celestial knowledge. I also wanted to introduce readers to some fundamental principles of Vedic philosophy that support astrology. The concepts of Vedic thought are very fascinating, and in many respects are "out of this world" for those new to it. However, a little bit of Vedic philosophy will enrich your comprehension of the amazing field of Vedic astrology.

I didn't want this book to be too dense or text heavy, which is certainly a challenge when your goal is to convey all the pertinent Vedic material! I wanted to cover the basics and pique your interest as readers, but leave the more detailed explanations to other books, such as my introductory work, *Beneath a Vedic Sky*. I've also made a conscious decision, as in most of my writings, not to take up too much time and space with chart examples. This is the convention in ancient Jyotish writings—learn the principles, practice with real-life examples, and the knowledge will pour forth. I've tried to set things up so that you can validate what you've learned through your own charts, which you can create on the enclosed CD-ROM software, Parashara's Light SE.

Again, I'm intending to give you a rich yet simplified overview of Vedic astrology. It's my hope that the bright scholars of the Vedas will accept this well-intended overview and that the beginning readers of this book won't find it too complex. I want to show you how to tell time, but not how to make a watch! Most of all, I hope you find this book fascinating and fun—and as I always say, don't try too hard to understand. Stay relaxed and the knowledge will come in time.

A COMPARISON
OF VEDIC AND
WESTERN SYSTEMS

S ome of you will begin this book with a familiarity with tropical astrology (as is mostly practiced in the West), so I think it may be helpful to inform you about some of the differences between the astrology of the West and that of the *Vedas* (vay' dahs), from the East.

First let me state that indicating the differences between Vedic and tropical astrology isn't to say that one system is better than the other. The intention here is to help you understand some of the key components of the Vedic method that stand apart from the Western approach. This summary will give you a high-level overview before you plunge into the core of the book.

1. Different Start Dates for the Sun Signs: No, your Western Sun sign didn't disappear! The Vedic system starts at the first point of the sign (and constellation) of Aries around April 14 each year, and the Vedic Sun signs transition around the second week each month—not the third, as in the tropical.

The Western system is a zodiac of *signs*. The Vedic system is a zodiac of *constellations*. As such, each system starts its zodiac on different days. You'll notice in the following table that the two systems overlap around the second to third week of each month (about the 15th to the 20th, plus or minus a day or two). If you were born during that time, your Sun sign would be the same in either system; otherwise, your Sun sign will move back one sign in the Vedic system. This is due to *precession,* which will be discussed in a bit.

No.	Rasi (Vedic names)	Signs (Western names)	Sidereal (Vedic astrological calendar)	Tropical (Western astrological calendar)
1.	Mesha	Aries	Apr 13–May 14	Mar 21–Apr 21*
2.	Vrishabha	Taurus	May 15–Jun 14	Apr 22–May 20
3.	Mithuna	Gemini	Jun 15–Jul 14	May 21–Jun 21
4.	Karka	Cancer	Jul 15–Aug 14	Jun 22–Jul 22
5.	Simha	Leo	Aug 15–Sep 15	Jul 23–Aug 23
6.	Kanya	Virgo	Sep 16–Oct 15	Aug 24–Sep 23
7.	Tula	Libra	Oct 16–Nov 14	Sep 24–Oct 23
8.	Vrishchika	Scorpio	Nov 15–Dec 14	Oct 24–Nov 22
9.	Dhanus	Sagittarius	Dec 15–Jan 13	Nov 23–Dec 21
10.	Makara	Capricorn	Jan 14–Feb 12	Dec 22–Jan 21
11.	Kumbha	Aquarius	Feb 13–Mar 12	Jan 22–Feb 19
12.	Meena	Pisces	Mar 13–Apr 12*	Feb 20–Mar 20

* Sign starting the new astrological year

2. Largest Astrological System: Due to the fact that India is the second most populous nation in the world at this time, and astrology is an integral and accepted part of their society, India most likely has the highest number of astrologers and clients per capita of any nation. A great many people in modern India—from priests, executives, and merchants, right down to the common worker (whether they'll admit it or not)—use astrology to some degree and recognize it as part of their ancient traditions.

3. Philosophical Integration: Vedic astrology is part of a large integrated system of philosophy called the *Veda*. The fundamental principles used in Vedic astrology can also be found linked to its sister systems, such as *Ayurveda,* the Science of Health; and *Vastu,* the Science of Space (a cousin to the popular Feng Shui system of placement).

4. Predictive Tools: Many people state that tropical astrology is focused more on psychological analysis. While this might be true, the Vedic system is also equipped to perform this function. However, the Vedic system has a very large set of predictive techniques that analyze and forecast events ranging in time from several seconds to several decades of life.

5. Tropical vs. Sidereal: Most Western astrology systems use a zodiac of signs related to seasons—that is, tropical, while the Eastern Vedic system uses a zodiac of constellations related to stars—that is, *sidereal* (sigh deer' ee all). Tropical astrology states that the signs are defined by the equinoctial and tropical points, especially the Sun's location at the vernal equinox. Vedic astrology says that the signs are marked by their proximity to the constellations that bear their names, thus striving to adjust the position of the signs to the constellations in reaction to precession.

6. Number of Planets: Traditional Vedic astrology uses the Sun and Moon and the planets up to and including Saturn. It doesn't use the slower moving, unseen (by the naked eye) outer planets of Uranus, Neptune, and Pluto. Vedic astrology also puts a special emphasis on the nodes of the Moon, called *Rahu* (rah' hoo) and *Ketu* (kay' too or keh' too). The Western system (as well as some modern Vedic astrologers) also use the outer planets of Uranus, Neptune, and Pluto. It's also important to note that Vedic astrology places more significance on the rising sign, called the *Lagna* (lahg' nah), and the Moon than it does to the Sun.

In Vedic astrology, the planets are listed in terms of their rulerships of the days of the week, starting with the Sun and "Sun" day, and ending with Saturn or "Satur[n]" day. The nodes don't rule any weekdays. It's also interesting to note that Vedic astrology considers a special set of auxiliary "planets," called *upagrahas* (oo' pah grah' hahs), for advanced chart analysis.

7. Chart Formats: The Vedic charts are square and are interpreted in a style that is different from the familiar round charts of Western systems.

8. Precession and Ayanamsa: About 1,700 years ago, around A.D 285 (according to Vedic scholar Lahiri and the Indian government), sidereal Aries and tropical Aries were marked approximately in the same position in the skies. Researchers will differ a bit about the actual date and marker point of the Aries sign/constellation alignment, but they all agree that the signs are slipping backward in relationship to

Saraswati (sar rah' swah tee), *Goddess of music and learning.*

the constellations at a rate of about one degree every 72 years. Due to this backward drift of Earth, called "precession of the equinoxes," the first point of Aries has precessed, or slipped back, from March 21 (the day of the Spring equinox) to later in the calendar year—around April 14. The Vedic system compensates for this precession. This 23- to 24-day difference between where the two systems mark the start of the sign of Aries is called the *Ayanamsa* (ah' yahn ahm' shah). Proponents of the tropical system say that the zodiac signs are seasonal segments of the heavens independent of the constellations, and thus they don't adjust for precession.

9. House Systems: The Western system has many house systems to divide up the zodiac, while the standard Vedic convention is to treat the house and sign of equal length—thus calling it the *equal house* system.

10. Aspects: Vedic astrology evaluates the favorableness of aspects differently from Western astrology. In the Vedic system, the quality and quantity of the influence of the participating planets is more important than assigning a value to the aspect itself.

11. Planetary Yogas: Planetary yogas are special combinations of planets that offer a degree of power and influence not seen in standard chart indications. There are literally hundreds of these combinations, pointing to "secret" planetary unions that reveal wealth, health, spiritual advancement, relationships, career success, and many other features of our lives not shown in standard chart analysis.

12. Nakshatras: In addition to the 12 signs of the zodiac, the Vedic system uses 27 "Moon signs," or additional nonzodiac asterisms, called the *nakshatras (*nahk shah' trahs). Each of the 27 nakshatras are subdivided into four sections, or *padas* (pah' dahs), thus making for 108 *nakshatra padas* in total.

13. Shodasavargas, the Divisional Charts: In addition to the familiar natal chart, Vedic astrology divides a sign of the zodiac 15 additional ways. The most famous of these divisions is called the *navamsa* (nahv ahm' shah), which divides a 30-degree zodiac sign into 9 subdivisions of 3 degrees and 20 minutes each. Thus the planets can be located in the 12 signs of the zodiac, and more precisely, within the 108 navamsas.

14. Dasas: The Vedic system has a way of forecasting when traits in the chart will show themselves through the use of a predictive analysis tool called the *vimshottari dasa* (vim shoh' tah ree dah' shah). This system allots each planet in the horoscope a specific period of influence in a person's hypothetical lifetime of 120 years.

15. Remedial Measures: The Vedic system not only identifies the results of karma in terms of the past, present, and future, but employs corrective measures, called *upayas* (oo pie' yahs), aimed at improving the quality and character of a person's life.

16. Additional Interpretive Techniques: There are many other methods of chart interpretation too numerous to mention in this small book, but as you read more detailed guides, such as my first astrology book, *Beneath a Vedic Sky,* you'll learn about *ashtakavarga* (ahsh' tahk ah var' gah), *varshaphal* (vahr' sha palh), *sudarshana chakra* (soo dahr' shah nah cha' krah), and other fascinating features of Vedic astrology.

17. Vedic Astrology as a Self-Development Tool: Since astrology is an integral part of the whole-systems approach of Vedic knowledge, the development of consciousness is regarded as a prerequisite for advancing one's skills as an astrologer. Traditional Vedic astrologers meditate, get proper rest, live and eat well, keep the company of the wise, and perform specific rituals and other special spiritual practices to become healthier and happier. They strive to develop the full capacity of their minds, bodies, and hearts. In this manner they can "see" nature more clearly and perform their work to their full potential.

18. Vedic Astrology as a Spiritual Performance: In traditional Vedic chart interpretation, the reading of a chart was conducted like a spiritual event. It would take place in a temple, where the priest/astrologer would draw the chart diagram and perform a small *puja,* or "ceremony," over the chart. Mantras would be recited and deities would be invoked to help make the reading a success. Even today, Hindu astrologers will recite mantras and invoke the help of their personal diety, called the *ishta devata,* to help them read the chart with reverence and accuracy . . . all undoubtedly helping the client get the best results!

Now that you know some of the distinctions between Vedic and tropical astrology, we'll move deeply, yet simply, into the principles and practices of Vedic astrology and its supporting Vedic systems of knowledge.

✤ ✤ ✤ ✤ ✤

Radha and Krishna symbolize the loving unity of the feminine and masculine principles in Vedic concepts of manifestation.

Surya, the Sun.

CHAPTER ONE

FOUNDATIONS OF VEDIC PHILOSOPHY

*As Space pervades a jar both in and out, similarly within and
beyond this ever changing universe, there exists one Universal Spirit.*
— Siva Samhita

Vedic thinkers inform us that the entirety of life's multiplicity is merged into an all-encompassing simplicity. The tapestry of life is stitched together by a unifying knowledge manifested from joy. There's an unchanging truth or order called *rita* (rih' tah) residing at the ground floor of all the laws of nature, and everything is an expression or "child" of that nourishing parent of wholeness. Some call it *satchitananda* (saht' chit' ah nahn' dah), which means "bliss consciousness." In contrast to the wheel of change, called *samsara* (sahm sah' rah), the concept of truth and joy permeates Vedic thinking. Everything in time and space is based on and energized by the infinite logic and boundless stability and joy of this order. It's a lovely "rita."

The Supreme organizing power of nature, experienced as *ananda* (ah nahn' dah), or "joy," invigorates the manifestation process, sustains, and renews . . . in essence, everything is one thing and if allowed to follow its nature, wants to return effortlessly to abide in joy. In a sense, we just have to stay out of the way by not getting too stressed. Everything is motivated by a desire to have more joy—be it getting a better job; creating more meaningful relationships; having more prosperity and health for ourselves, family, and friends; or attaining that mystical state of comfort called *enlightenment*. All of this is essentially That—

driven by the desire to be more of itself.

All the principles of Vedic astrology are tied to the concept of this unified field of knowledge. All the parts reflect the whole, and nothing stands alone—except our misconception of such, called *Maya*, or "that which is not." Thus, Vedic astrology finds the truth about events and people because it's an expression of the wholeness wanting to see itself. Vedic astrology practitioners are encouraged by tradition to live in a truthful manner and generate interpretations that reflect the "insight" and "in-joyment" that come from expressing from the mind of truth.

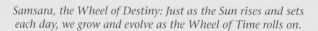

Samsara, the Wheel of Destiny: Just as the Sun rises and sets each day, we grow and evolve as the Wheel of Time rolls on.

Unity with the Divine

From the appreciation and desire to maintain order and balance and to reap its blessings, the concept of *yagya* (yagh' yuh), or "ritual offering," arose—enveloped in an atmosphere of praise and gratitude for life. Vedic priests developed specific rituals aimed at keeping life in order, and they worked to align and maintain the university within the diversity. At first, the aim of Vedic astrology (and its sibling, astronomy) was to help the priests determine the correct time to perform these important life-sustaining rituals. The stylized performances of the Veda kept the energy above and the life below linked in harmonious balance. People realized through the instruction and guidance of the priests and gurus that if they stayed orderly, calm, and joyful inside, then life around them—the laws of nature—would manifest in a similar manner. So not only was it "as above, so below," it was even more "as within, as without," because the world outside reflects our world inside. The world is as we are. Our feelings come from our focus; thus we improve our focus to improve our feelings.

So, the key was to gain the alliance of the laws of nature and become universal inside. The process was to offer praise-filled gifts and songs to the impulses of nature, which were essentially the impulses of human life. For some, this would seem to be an amazing complexity of mysticism. Yet for those who knew it well, it was nothing but the natural way to interact with the environment. We will see in our study of Vedic astrology coming up that maintaining a state of harmony with planetary energies, each ruled by a deity or *deva* (day' vah) or "shining one," was an important consideration in Vedic life.

Connecting the inner with the outer to form an integrated wholeness of life via Vedic ritual.

Time, Karma, and Reincarnation

The concept of order, *rita,* and the maintenance of a ritual-supported contract with nature gave rise to the theory of karma. The Vedic *rishis* (ree' shees) or "seers" understood that we're all responsible for our individual actions. *Kala* (kah' lah), or "time," is comprised of three elements—the past, present, and future. What happens to us, for the good or bad, is a result of what we've done in the past, what we are presently doing now, and what we intend to do in the future. Some people use the word *karma* to imply bad karma, but negative action is more appropriately called *dushkarma* (doosh' kar' mah). In the context of this book, karma is defined as "action," for the good or bad.

In a fundamental way, Vedic astrology is the study of karma. Vedic astrology calls the summary of one's past actions *sanchita* (sahn chih' tah) *karma,* as shown by the placements of planets in signs and houses and the interaction between these planets. The Vedic astrology chart also gives us an idea of our potential moving forward, both in terms of actions we take now, called *prarabdha* (prah rahb' dah) *karma,* and actions we intend to take in the future, called *agama* (ah gah' mah) *karma.* Some scholars break the karmas down into smaller sets, but these three are held by most to be the main classes.

Vedic philosophy also tells us that time is cyclical. It's not a straight, unending path into the future, comprised of millions of calendar years, but is a recursive or looping phenomenon that involves creation, maintenance, and dissolution. Time curves back on itself and creation occurs again and again like a big wheel of samsara that keeps on turning.

*The balance of good or bad Karma
brought forward from the previous
birth is prarabdha and it is the reading of
this that goes under the name
of Astrology.*
— Prasna Marga

The theory of karma tells us that all living beings are born according to their past actions. What you are now is a result of what you have done before. Good deeds, good life; bad deeds . . . well, you know the result. In one school of Vedic thought, it's said that some beings can undertake as many as 84,000 *yonis* (yoh' nees), or "births." We use the word *being* instead of *person* because the theory holds that all of these births might not be in human form. According to Vedic scholars, it's considered a rare thing to obtain human birth. Enlightened gurus tell us that such a gift must be treated with great reverence, joy, and focus—even if we feel a bit topsy-turvy at times. Our human consciousness is capable of amazing things and tremendous growth. It's a worthy investment to spend time developing our full potential and taking some time to celebrate our little bit of time on this Earth (at least for this go-round!).

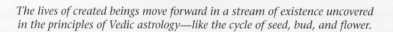

*The lives of created beings move forward in a stream of existence uncovered
in the principles of Vedic astrology—like the cycle of seed, bud, and flower.*

FREE WILL AND DESTINY

To paraphrase Nehru, modern India's first president, fate is the hand of cards that you've been dealt, and destiny is how you play them. You can see so many people who were given a bunch of lemons in this life and turned them into lemonade. Destiny is negotiable, but you have to be aware and knowledgeable in order to make the right choices. Astrology helps with that. The future is inevitable; it's always present. There's a natural order to things, but they aren't necessarily fixed. Through the tools of Vedic astrology you can transform your destiny into a good future through taking a better course of action now and looking at your past in a more constructive manner. We'll be discussing the concept of remedial measures later in the book. These are a means for a person to correct their course and develop a new style of action that leads to more positive outcomes.

MOKSHA: LIBERATION

. . . as from a blazing fire sparks proceed, living souls originate
from the indestructible Brahman and return to Him.
— Mundaka Upanishad

7

When astrologers' minds are full of light, they have more illumination to see what's happening around them—on the outside and the inside of Nature.

Vedic thought focuses a lot on the concept of *moksha* (mohk' shah), or "liberation." What does this mean exactly? Liberation from what? The term implies that we need to be freed or delivered from something that's holding us back. It's telling us that we need to unfasten or let go of something, that has caught us or is holding us fast—like some cosmic noose. Then we ask, "Held back from what?"

Liberation means that we're relieved from the stress of caring out of proportion to a context or event. Liberated people often state that they've learned to enjoy the "ordinariness" of things. While they remain responsible and vigilant, they say in some form or another, "Let thy will be done," "It doesn't matter," "Forget about it," "I don't mind," or similar statements showing acceptance. They're engaged in life, but not so irritated by it. However, they're not passive, as shown in some stereotypes.

Some people who I think are highly evolved—if not enlightened—are really dynamic, calm, and joy-filled people. They work hard without straining. Heroes and saints display this quality, and even some high-level executives, but it's within the reach of ordinary folks as well. It's just that the "enlightened" ones aren't overshadowed or hypersensitive about the external limitations or restraints seen around them. The light stays on inside. They have an inner momentum of illumination that isn't thrown off or slowed down by the apparent darkness of certain activities. They find joy, believe they are supported, and don't worry about it. They think in terms of all possibilities and anticipate positive outcomes, so they're able to respond and find a way to make things work within joy.

VALUE OF MEDITATION

Vedic practices for self-realization emphasize that liberation is achieved by having an experience of it, rather than merely intellectualizing or reading about it. This is why meditation is so important. Meditation is really a self-soothing strategy that doesn't have negative side effects, such as is experienced with overeating, drug and alcohol abuse, or other semi-adaptive attempts to maneuver past stress and strain. These inept soothing strategies might feel good on the front end, but they aren't so good on the back end. In Vedic literature, such things are called "double-dealing *rakshasas* (rock shah' sahs), a personalized, unreliable form of negative energy.

After a number of experiences of that state of inner peace and creativity, we begin to realize that this is the natural state of all life. Eventually the dip into the sea of joyfulness saturates us and it becomes an established blissful habit of the mind, experienced 24 hours a day without being overshadowed by the ups and downs of daily life. Stress might come, but it's like a line drawn on water—it quickly dissolves away and we're soon back to our Self.

UNITY OF THE SEXES

Another important aspect of unity in Vedic philosophy is that male and female forces are not opposed—in fact, they're an integrated unit of life where one depends on and supplements the other. They comply with each other. The goddess element is very important in Vedic thinking, and each male deity has no *Shakti* (shahk' tee), or "power," without his female counterpart. While the male takes action, he gets his

The Vedic roles of male and female work as an integrated partnership of wholeness, not a battle of the sexes with attention to differences and reluctance to negotiate or submit to one another.

power from the female. They collaborate and don't try to have their own way too much. A good image of this is seen in the Goddess *Kali* (kah' lee) dancing on the body of *Shiva* (shee' vah), reminding him that without her, he is dead.

THE BALANCE OF GOOD AND EVIL

The unity or balance of seemingly opposing forces is represented in the celestial battles of the *devas,* the forces of good, against the *asuras* (ah suhr' ahs), the forces of evil. Psychologists tell us today that one of our biggest tasks as humans is to learn how to resolve opposites. Many tales in Vedic scripture personify the battle of good versus evil as the conflict between these heavenly and demonic forces. The idea is to bring the positive forces into our lives and have them in greater proportion than the destructive ones. This brings health and happiness, which is why it's also a key concept in Ayurveda, India's health system.

Much of Vedic ritual is involved in propitiating or pleasing the devas, or positive elemental forces. The aim is to gain their support for building a bountiful life on earth, both on the inside and outside. It's cosmic teamwork—we praise them, they help us.

The devas, here represented as the Seven Matrikas (mah' tree kahs)
or Divine Mothers, in battle with the asuras, the forces of evil.

CORRELATION OF NATURE AND THE BODY

In this body . . . there are seers and sages; all the stars and planets as well.
The Sun and Moon, agents of creation and destruction, also move in it.
Ether, Air, Fire, Water, and Earth are there also.
— Shiva Samhita

Vedic astrology gives us further evidence that we're united with nature. This is manifest in the signs of the zodiac identified with certain parts of the body. The cosmos is replicated within the individual—in other words, we are full of stars. Some tantric scholars indicate that the celestial Moon sits at the top of our spinal column, raining down its milky rays, and the Sun radiates its dawning, vivifying light up from the base of the spine—both working day and night to fill us with light and health.

As we look above at the mechanics of the celestial realms, we see their correspondence within the physiology of created beings. The chart shows all the areas of life related to planetary indicators. We don't necessarily say the planets *cause* things to happen as much as they indicate patterns of nature that tend to produce certain results over time . . . just like using statistical information to identify trends and forecast events. The meteorologist's charts don't cause the rainstorms, but those dripping cloud diagrams we see on TV tell us that we have a certain probability of afternoon showers. We also see this concept of the unity of the above with the below in similar patterns of matching planets and constellations to markings on the body—most specifically with the lines of the hand, as practiced in *Rekha Shastra* (reh' kah shah' strah) or "palmistry." Everything is connected to everything else.

The impulses of nature are the same everywhere, and can be seen expressed not only in celestial mechanics, but in terms of how our bodies work within the integrated construct of nature, as revealed by the principles of Vedic astrology.

GUIDANCE OF THE GURU

One of the principal ways in which Vedic knowledge is passed down over the ages is through the agency of the guru, the cosmic coach. The guru is a concrete example of living from a state of boundless joy and all possibilities. Gurus walk the talk and expound on knowledge to help alleviate the doubts and confusion of the students. They're adept at providing their students with various experiences, such as meditation coupled with dynamic action, to speed them on their way to liberation or self-sufficiency. They offer a balanced distraction, so their disciples get removed from obsessing on doubt and thereby gain more traction with the Self. The students seek and support the guru, and the guru is compelled by the students' sincerity to share the lessons learned on the roadless road to the Self.

The guru as mentor gives the disciple a concrete example of how to live easily and powerfully in a more healthy and happy manner—100 percent in the spiritual world and 100 percent in the material world.

THE FOUR CASTES

The concept of order in Vedic society was further expressed in the hierarchy of social purpose called the *varnas* (var' nahs), which we know today as the "caste system." What Westerners understand of the caste system today isn't what was originally intended. For India, these four categories of labor were believed to have been passed down to man from Brahma himself, and their purpose was to give structure for balanced growth in society. Everyone was honored, rewarded, and recognized for the appropriate action they performed. By acting according to their nature and *dharma,* or "right action," the nation prospered and orderly life in the cosmos was upheld.

The four castes are as follows:

Brahmins (brah' mins): The priest and philosopher class charged with ritual and instruction

Kshatriyas (kshah' tree ahs): The executive and warrior class responsible for managing and protecting

Vaishyas (vy' shyahs): The merchant class focused on the affairs of commerce and trade

Sudras (soo' drahs): The servant class who labor and serve the needs of the other three classes

THE ROLE OF VEDIC MYTH AND TYPES OF VEDIC LITERATURE

The ancient astronomers/astrologers used myth as their tool to capture and record the fundamental mechanics of nature. All the aspects of the natural world were embedded in the emotional and behavioral characteristics, customs, and ideals represented by stories. There were no scientific formulas or rule books as we know them today—only legends. The mythmakers personified the forces of nature and represented them as a body of supernatural celestial beings, revered ancestors, or inspiring role-model heroes capable of astounding feats in the destruction of evil.

Veda comes from the Sanskrit word *vid,* or "knowledge." Our English word *vision* is derived from this ancient root word. After all, knowledge is a way of seeing the world, and we see what we know. Many scholars contend that the Vedas are the oldest known set of scriptures available in the world. They were a way of knowing generated from the visions of rishis (sages). There is a belief that sage Veda Vyasa (vya' sah) played a major role in collecting the primary Vedic oral works, gathering them into volumes called *samhitas* (sam hee' tahs). The principal works compiled by Vyasa, around the third millennium B.C., were the four major Vedas: *Rig* (rigk), *Sama* (sah' mah), *Atharva* (ah tahr' vah), and *Yajur* (yah' joor), as well as the *Brahma Sutras* (soo' trahs), the *Mahabharata* (mah' hah bhah rah' tah), and the 18 *Puranas* (puhr rahn' ahs). It's said that Vyasa comes each Vedic time period (called a *Kali Yuga)* to recompile the Vedas.

While the four Vedas contain the basic Hindu rituals, modes of worship, mantras, and the fundamental social and religious principles, the *Upanishads* (oop pahn' ih shads) were created to expound on the essential philosophical secrets embedded in the Vedas. In fact, the Upanishads are sometimes called *Vedanta* (vay dhan' tah), which means the "end of the Veda," signifying that they contain the final fruit or essence of the main Vedic texts. Most scholars hold that there are 108 Upanishads, and out of this repository of knowledge, 12 principal Upanishads are key, carrying names such as *Taitiriya* (tie' tir ee yah), *Mundaka* (moon dah' kah), *Chandogya* (cahn dohg' yah), and *Brihad-Aranyaka* (bree' hahd ah rahn' yah kah).

The ancient Vedic rishis didn't identify the fundamentals of Vedic astrology using telescopes and other instruments, but cognized celestial principles from within their heightened awareness.

The Vedic astrologer uses the principles of Jyotish, the light of nature, to see into the affairs of people, places, and things in terms of the past, present, and future.

Another very popular scripture, called the *Bhagavad Gita* (bah' gah vahd gee' tah), the "Song of God," is taken from the larger work of the *Mahabharata,* a classic Hindu epic. The Gita, as it's affectionately called, carries some of the core precepts of Vedic thought.

Finally, it's good to draw attention to the *Yogasutras* (yoh' gah soo' trahs) of Patanjali (pah tahn' jah lee). This classic of Vedic literature explains the philosophy of gaining liberation through yoga practices and thought strengthening formulas called *siddhis* (sih' dees), or "perfections." Patanjali's work, coupled with his yoga and meditation routines, offers extremely good knowledge about how the mind operates as it moves to enlightenment.

Cognition of the Rishis

In Sanskrit, the word *sanskrita* (sahn skrih' tah) means "refined" or "sanctified." It's used with the Sanskrit word *vak* (vahk), which means "speech" or "language," so we see that the developers of Sanskrit considered it a holy language. In fact, it's called the Language of the Gods. Believers hold that the knowledge contained in the Veda is *apaurusheya* (ah pah roo' shay ah)—that is, it wasn't created by humans, or *purusha* (poo roo' shah). The knowledge of the Veda, which is essentially the mechanics of creation, was perceived from the level of pure awareness of ancient rishis (seers). This segment of Vedic knowledge is called *shruti* (shroo' tee) or "heard," in that this knowledge was directly perceived through the expanded awareness of these original wise men. This shruti level of knowledge developed into a system of oral teaching that was supported by the guru-disciple traditions of India over many thousands of years.

VEDIC ASTROLOGY: THE EYE OF THE VEDA

As the oral teachings began to be written down, this new phase of Vedic knowledge came to be called *smriti* (smrih' tee), or "remembered." To augment the correct study of the Veda, a set of auxiliary works were built around the original four Vedas. There are six major categories of supplemental knowledge called the *vedangas* (vay dahng' ahs), or "branches," of the Veda. Each of these works are identified with a part of the body of the *Cosmic Purusha,* wherein the entire universe is depicted as the human body. The eyes of the Purusha were called *Jyotish,* from the Sanskrit root *jyotir* (jyoh' teer), meaning "light," and *ish* from *ishwara* (eesh wahr' ah), or "nature"—also translated as "God in the form of all-nature."

Thus Jyotish is called "the eye of the Veda." It's deemed as the awareness that can see the universal order of life in terms of the past, present, and future. A practitioner of Jyotish is called a *Jyotishi* (jyoh tee' shee), or in modern terms, a Vedic astrologer. It's the task of the Jyotishi to apply the principles and practices of the light of nature in order to know the flow of karma over time. Their eye becomes the eye of nature that can "see" the past, present, and future of a person. The astrologers work their craft in terms of specific diagrams called *bha chakras* (bah chah' krahs), or "light wheels," which are calculated from the time and place of a person's birth. We also refer to these as horoscopes, birth charts, or natal charts.

The Jyotishis follow very specific rules of astrology chart construction and interpretation believed to have been passed down from Vedic deities such as Brahma (the creator god) to sages, such as Parashara. In fact, Parashara's book *Brihat* (bree' haht) *Parashara* (pah rah' shah rah') *Hora* (hohr' ah) *Shastra* (shahs' trah) is believed by

Saraswati, Goddess of Learning, prayed to by traditional Vedic astrologers to increase the clarity of their chart interpretations.

many to be the "Bible" of Jyotish knowledge. Many other sages followed Parashara, such as *Varahamihira* (vah rah' hah mee heer' ah), *Garga* (gahr' gah), and *Satyacharya* (saht' yah chah' ree yah), making Vedic astrology more accessible to the general population. The books deemed to have been written by rishis themselves, called *rishi prokta* (prohk' tah), are considered the most authoritative.

Until recent times, Jyotish was most often referred to in English as "Indian" or "Hindu" astrology. In the early '80s, gurus such as Maharishi Mahesh Yogi began calling it Vedic astrology, which is generally what it's referred to as in this book. The name *Vedic astrology* was further embedded into the language of the West through the efforts of organizations such as the American College of Vedic Astrology, led by Dr. Dennis Harness, and the Council of Vedic Astrology, under the leadership of Dennis Flaherty. Modern pundits, such as Dr. B. V. Raman and his *Astrological Magazine,* along with his editor daughter, Gayatri Devi Vasudev, and publisher son, Niranjan Babu, have also helped popularize the astrology of India for Western readers.

❀ ❀ ❀ ❀ ❀

The author with the late Dr. B. V. Raman
at his home in Bangalore, India.

Chandra, the Moon.

CHAPTER TWO

FUNDAMENTALS OF VEDIC ASTROLOGY

*Whatever auspiciousness or inauspiciousness one has earned in the
last birth due to one's various deeds will be known through the science
of astrology, just as the lamp throws light on the articles in darkness.*
— Varahamihira

THE PURPOSE OF ASTROLOGY

Astrology is the study of karma, which is action and reaction, in terms of the past, present, and future. It observes the interplay of beings within the field of space and time. Astrology works to identify behavior, forecast outcomes, and suggest preventive measures via a systematic process. It bases its high rate of predictability on a specific set of measurements derived from the celestial mechanics of astronomy.

Astrologers endeavor to uncover the correct times to undertake events for maximum effect, or to identify those periods in which it might be better to avoid action in order to avert a negative outcome. Astrology draws on the mathematics and observations of astronomy, and it uses these scientific tools as a means of analyzing and measuring behavioral patterns over time, as well as forecasting trends.

Astrology was most likely the first statistical analysis tool. Today's social scientists do a lot of forecasting or trend analysis using statistics in a field called *predictive analytics*. Using esoteric processes, such as data mining and the like, these modern tools deliver results that parallel those of Vedic astrology techniques. Analysis is performed on the data of current and past conditions to draw reliable and valid conclusions. This enables users of the analysis to perform more effective action moving forward. The insights gained by the analysis also helps its users understand how others might be inclined to behave in terms of their characteristics, skills, interests, and attitudes.

So astrology's founders were, in a sense, cosmic statisticians of celestial and terrestrial events. In addition to their original cognitions of nature's operations, they gathered data and took many measurements over the millennia, designing astrology as a predictive system. All this knowledge was embedded in classical texts and within the principles and practices of the craft of astrology. As forecasters, astrologers have learned to effectively approximate or calculate events in advance, through the analysis of astronomical data, in conjunction with specific astrological principles.

At first glance, the principles related to the structure and origin of the skies above might seem to be different from that of the world below. However, at their core the functions of the stellar regions were found to be similar in function to the patterns of nature on the Earth. The impulses that drive human behavior are, in essence, the same as those that impel the dance of the planets. The skies above, with their celestial denizens, and the creatures below moving on the earth were related enough to permit inferences between the two. They were singing from the same songbook . . . the song of life.

THE ROLE OF THE ASTROLOGER

If the mind of the astrologer is steady, and the person to whom the future is read is humble and devout in temperament, then the reading will be correct and the answer to all the questions will be invariably good. If the astrologer is calm, if the querent frames his question in the proper form . . . then the questioner will attain his desired object.
— Prasna Marga, Method of Reading the Results, Stanzas 14 and 15

The astrologer observes the patterns of life seen in the workings of nature, especially astronomy, and transfers this integrated knowledge into a past, present, and future review of a person's life via the birth chart.

Astrologers are the sentinels of time. They help their clients understand their past actions and how the results of these events will potentially unfold over time. How well this happens is also in accord with the context of a person's environment, the level of their reasonable expectations and desire to change, along with the "good credit" or *punya* (poon' yah) they have built up to the current time. In order to identify special events in a client's life and determine how their behavior might unfold over time, the astrologer creates a

With developed consciousness, the Vedic astrologer can perceive the mechanics of nature through the traits assigned to planets and analyze tendencies of behavior and forecast events using the principles and practices of Vedic astrology.

horoscope, or birth chart, which is a map of what the sky looked like for a person's time and place of birth. The astrologer is trained to match patterns of basic horoscope models to what they see in the birth chart. The database and rules from which they draw their knowledge is thousands of years old.

In our modern times, the astrologer most likely uses a software program to calculate the horoscope, such as is included in this book. This program computes the position of planets in signs and houses of the zodiac and identifies the interaction of the planets in the chart. Following prescribed astrological principles and procedures for forecasting the future, based on past patterns, the astrologer analyzes the birth chart or horoscope.

The astrologer informs clients, hopefully in a truthful yet comforting manner, as to the possible direction of future trends and events. They alert these clients, without alarming them, on how to avoid or reduce dangerous life events. Without too much cheerleading, the experienced astrologer helps clients understand how to promote positive actions at the appropriate period of time.

DEVELOPMENT OF CONSCIOUSNESS— THE KEY TO GOOD ASTROLOGY

After some time, astrologers come to realize that they don't *do* astrology as much as they *become* astrology. While no one in this material world can predict anything with 100 percent accuracy, seasoned astrologers are able to harvest much of the *phalita dasa* (pahl' lee tah dah' shah), or "fruits of time," contained in the birth chart. They're able to do this in proportion to the advances they've made with their cognitive abilities and intuition. Vedic astrology is a state of consciousness as well as a set of principles, and one of the benefits of being a Vedic astrologer over time is the development of consciousness that comes from constant attention to the practice. As we know, what we put our attention on grows stronger over time.

To put our minds on the universality of time in the past, present, and future creates a state of boundlessness in the mind of the knowledgeable and dedicated Jyotishi. Some of these advanced states of awareness are called *trikala gyana* (tree' kah lah gyah' nah), the "knowledge of the three times," *deva drishti* (drish' tee), or "divine sight," and most important, *Jyotish mati pragya* (mah' tee prahg' yah), or that state of mind that sees the light and *is* the light.

Any serious student of Vedic astrology knows it's good to receive *diksha* (dihk'shah), or "initiation," from a bona fide guru and practice daily meditation to improve creativity, mental clarity, and to free the mind and body of stress and strain. Meditation helps develop the average astrologer into that class of Jyotishis who have a higher level of intuition and insight into the secrets of determining behavior over time.

The Role of the Client

*Only humble requests deserve an answer. No prediction should be offered to
a person unasked for, nor to one who wishes to test the astrologer. If the
astrologer attempts to answer him, he will not be able to get at the truth.*
— Prasna Marga

One should not approach the astrologer empty-handed.
— Prasna Marga

Skilled astrologers understand that while clients want direction, they don't necessarily want to follow it. In this regard, the responsibility for the outcome of the session transfers to the client. One of the first tasks of a person seeking an astrological consultation is to locate a genuine Vedic astrologer. Getting a good referral from someone you know will help ensure that you have a good session. Once you have arranged your session and are interacting with the astrologer, it's important to put forth your questions in a respectful and positive manner. Doing so will help you attract and keep the attention of the astrologer. You wouldn't want to insult your doctor right before surgery; likewise, a positive interaction with the astrologer will enable you to have a fruitful consultation.

Also, when you decide to engage in an astrological consultation, you'll want to do a readiness review. Ask yourself how prepared you really are for change and how reasonable your expectations might be about that. Many clients come for direction, but they don't necessarily want to follow any advice. You need to determine whether you believe that change is really possible or not, and that you're ready to change now. If you don't do anything differently, or introduce new behaviors, then nothing much will change for you after your astrology session. You have to really assess what you're willing to exchange for a new future. If you want a new crop, you have to plant new seeds . . . and you have to pull those weeds early!

Vedic Principles Underlying Vedic Astrology

Vedic scholars tell us that there's an underlying field to existence called *Brahman,* which comes from the Sanskrit root *brahm,* meaning "to expand" or "to grow." The basic nature of Brahman is to expand *ananda*—"joy." He is joy and wants to be more of himself. Out of the unity or wholeness of Brahman springs forth all the diversity of life . . . and everything loops back to That in the grand *lila* (lee' lah) or "play" of nature. All the *Gopis* (goh' pees) or "cow maidens" want to come back to Krishna, the original cowboy!

In the Vedic theory of manifestation, Brahman sits at the foundation of life and is sometimes considered as the sound *Om,* the *Shabda* (shahb' dah) *Brahman,* or "first sound of life." From this first word or creative vibration is generated the three basic operations of *prakriti* (prah' kruh tee), or "nature," called the *gunas* (goo' nahs). *Guna* means a "strand of rope" in Sanskrit and signifies how nature is "tied together" at this fundamental level of manifestation. The gunas are originally in a state of balance, but when divinely irritated or stirred, they start the interactions of creation. First, there is *sattva* (saht' vah) guna, which signifies the quality of goodness and the maintenance of balance in life. Sattva guna is represented by the deity *Vishnu,* who is called "The

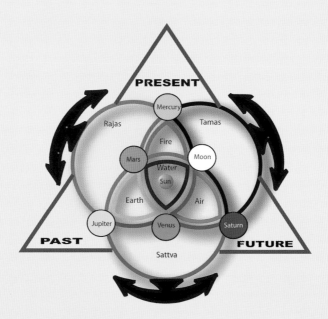

All the principles of Vedic astrology form an integrated whole wherein the Vedic astrologer uses astronomy, time, and place in a systematic manner to analyze behavior, capture trends, and forecast events.

Preserver." Second, life is manifested through the agency of *rajas* (rah' jahs) guna, which give us energy and spurs us on to engage in activity. Brahma represents the quality of rajas. The third guna is *tamas* (tah' mahs), which represents stability, stillness, and cessation. *Shiva,* the Destroyer and the Lord of Silence, represents tamas guna.

After the three gunas are stirred up, they combine further to form the five basic *bhutas* (bhoo' tahs), or "elements" of life. The elements form a common strand of

Brahma is rajas, the Creator.

five threads. These weave in and out of all Vedic systems, such as Jyotish, the Science of Time; Ayurveda, the Science of Health; and Vastu, the Science of Space. Each bhuta has a planet associated with it, as shown in the preceding list. The planets carry the characteristics of these elements, among other things. For example, Mars is a fiery, aggressive planet indicated by it association with the element of fire.

The gunas combine and the elements develop from them as manifestation progresses. In this process, the elements combine further and we experience the formation of the planets, called the *grahas* (grah' hahs), or "graspers," in Vedic astrology.

Ether/Akasha (ah kah' shah): Jupiter represents creativity, ingenuity, and mental agility.

Fire/Tejas (tay' jahs) or **Agni** (ahg' nee): The Sun, Mars, and Ketu represent energy, aggression, and executive ability.

Earth/Bhoomi (boo' mee) or **Prithivi** (prih tee' vee): Mercury represents focus, dedication, and devotion.

Air/Vayu (vah' yoo): Saturn and Rahu represent mobility and a mental orientation.

Shiva is tamas, the Dissolver.

Vishnu is sattva, the Preserver, keeping the Universe going with every breath.

Water/Apa (ah' pah) or **Jala** (jah' lah): The Moon and Venus represent emotions, intuition, and flexibility of mind.

The planets are the key to astrology. As you start examining a chart, you'll see that the building blocks, or basic components of chart interpretation, are as follows:

- Planets
- Signs
- Houses
- Interactions and modifications of planets aspecting each other in signs and houses

Your initial task as an astrologer is to evaluate the strengths and weaknesses (quantity of influence) and the favorableness or unfavorableness (quality of influences) of the planets in their natural state and judge how their basic nature is modified in response to where they're located in signs and houses, and how they interact and are modified via their aspects (the angular space or distance between planets).

In the next chapter, we'll examine the Vedic concept of *grahas,* or planets.

The five elements have an integrated function in all Vedic systems, including Ayurveda, optimum health; and Vastu, optimal dwelling places.

Kuja, the planet Mars.

CHAPTER THREE

GRAHAS: THE VEDIC PLANETS

The unborn Lord has many incarnations. He has incarnated, as the
Navagrahas (Nine Planets) to bestow on living beings the results due to their
karmas. He is Janardana (rewarder of past deeds). He assumed the auspicious form
of planets to destroy the asuras (evil forces) and sustain the devas (positive forces).
— Brihat Parashara Hora Shastra, Chapter 2

Technically speaking, there is no word in Sanskrit for "planet" as it's used in English. The term for a planet is actually *graha,* which means "to grasp" or "to hold." Each planet, according to the quality and quantity of influence it has in a specific chart, holds certain indications of behavior. Some would say the planets grasp our destiny. The planets deliver our inclination to act in favorable or unfavorable ways over time, and each planet is a messenger of our past actions and is the gateway to our tendency to act in a particular way in the future. A planet's natural tendencies are modified by its position in a chart—that is, within signs and houses of the zodiac. This is a very important principle to keep in mind while interpreting a chart.

A planet's location in a sign shows its strength or weakness, and its position in various houses indicates if it will deliver favorable or unfavorable effects as the result of our previous actions. Planets generally rule, or give their characteristics to, two signs (except the Sun and Moon). The malefic (unpleasant) or benefic (pleasant) disposition of each planet shows the manner in which our karma might tend to unfold over the course of this lifetime. We must remember that Vedic astrology judgments aren't fatalistic, although some astrologers who are still developing the fullness of their personalities might fall into this fixed line of thinking. Vedic astrology contends that a person can perform certain corrective actions and counterbalance negative deeds, thus moving forward into a more evolved state of existence. There's hope for us all!

The planets formed from a field of light that the Vedic seers called hiranyagarba, or the "Golden Womb." These subtle forces gradually condensed out of this field into balls of space and time that grasped ("graha") or pulled in matter to form the dense planets and solar system.

Cosmogenesis

We can also look at the graha representing a point in the solar system that contains specific forms of energy and influence. This concept has interesting parallels in modern Western theories of cosmogenesis, or solar system formation. Astrophysicists believe that the solar system started out as a large stellar cloud of dust and gas. Reacting to some energizing stimulation, perhaps the shockwave of a nearby nova explosion, the cloud was activated. (Vedic thinkers say that Brahman had a thought of Himself, thereby creating the condition of an observer, the observed, and an act of observation, thus manifesting the duality of time and space from within Himself.) The stellar cloud began to move and slowly started to rotate.

The laws of astrophysics came into play, and the center of the cloud started to heat up. At certain points in the slowly spinning disk (looking somewhat like Vishnu's discus), matter began to congeal. These points of coalescence, somewhere between the inner pull of the center of the young solar system and the outer pull of centrifugal force, began to grasp matter and become recognizable as protoplanets. Eventually, these specific points in the spin of the solar system formation became what we today call full-fledged planets.

The planets interact with their neighboring planets in specific ways—they gain strength and favorableness according to where they're positioned in the path of the zodiac (signs), in relationship to the Earth (houses), and how far they are from each other (aspects). The interactions within the solar system form a mandala of activity.

The grahas were identified by the seers, such as Parashara, as possessing specific inclinations and traits of behavior. These characteristics were documented in Vedic literature and within the identity and myths of celestial beings. The personalities of the graha deities exemplified the characteristics of the planets they were said to rule or govern.

In the Vedic system, there are nine planets, along with 12 signs and houses of the zodiac. The nine planets are the Sun, Moon, Mars, Mercury, Jupiter, Venus, Saturn, Rahu, and Ketu (notice that the first seven planets are identified with and follow the order of the days of the week). In traditional Vedic astrology, the outer planets of Uranus, Neptune, and Pluto aren't considered, although some researchers point to some Vedic scriptures, such as the *Mahabharata,* that identify celestial bodies that might actually be these three planets.

RELATIONSHIP BETWEEN PLANETS

The key components of Vedic astrology are planets, signs, houses, and the conjunctions and aspects between planets as they reside in the various signs and houses. The standard planetary aspects are one (conjunctions) and seven away (oppositions). Remember to start counting aspects considering the first sign or house as number one.

Conjunctions are planets located anywhere together in the same sign of the zodiac. Conjunctions occur only within the sign in Vedic astrology. There is no specific degree of proximity (orb) required to create an aspect. However, the closer the planets are to each other, the more their influences can be seen.

Oppositions are from planets separated by 180 degrees, or seven signs.

Vedic astrology also has the following special planetary aspects:

- **Mars** aspects other planets 4 and 8 houses away.

- **Jupiter** throws an aspect 5 and 9 houses ahead.

- **Saturn** casts a special glance at planets 3 and 10 houses from itself.

- Some authors, such as Parashara, indicate that **Rahu and Ketu** aspect houses 5 and 9 from themselves.

Planet	Natural Benefic or Malefic	Rulership	Own Sign(s), Swakshetra	Parashara's Exaltation Sign/ Degree Uucha	Parashara's Debilitation Sign/Degree Neecha	Moola-trikona Sign
Sun	Malefic	Leo	Leo 20 to 30	Aries 10	Libra 10	Leo 0 to 20
Moon	Benefic	Cancer	Cancer	Taurus 3	Scorpio 3	Cancer 3 to 30

THE STRENGTH OF PLANETS BY POSITION WITHIN SIGNS OF THE ZODIAC

Planet	Natural Benefic or Malefic	Rulership	Own Sign(s), Swakshetra	Parashara's Exaltation Sign/ Degree Uucha	Parashara's Debilitation Sign/Degree Neecha	Moola-trikona Sign
Mars	Malefic	Aries & Scorpio	Aries 12 to 30 & Scorpio	Capricorn 28	Cancer 28	Aries 0 to 12
Mercury	Benefic	Virgo & Gemini	Virgo 20 to 30 & Gemini	Virgo 15	Pisces 15	Virgo 15 to 20
Jupiter	Benefic	Sagittarius & Pisces	Sagittarius 10 to 30 & Pisces	Cancer 5	Capricorn 5	Sagittarius 0 to 10
Venus	Benefic	Taurus & Libra	Taurus 15 to 30 & Libra	Pisces 27	Virgo 27	Libra 0 to 15
Saturn	Malefic	Aquarius & Capricorn	Aquarius 20 to 30 & Capricorn	Libra 20	Aries 20	Aquarius 0 to 20
Rahu	Malefic	Virgo	Virgo	Taurus	Scorpio	None
Ketu	Malefic	Pisces	Pisces	Scorpio	Taurus	None

Rulerships: Each planet rules or is the "lord" of a particular sign or signs. Usually there's some similarity in the meaning and characteristic traits between the sign and its ruler. If you know what the planet means, you have a good head start in knowing about the sign it rules. For example, look at the signs of Virgo and Gemini as Mercury's signs. If Saturn is located in Virgo (ruled by Mercury), one could say that the planet Saturn is in Mercury's sign, indicating that there's a relationship of the planet Saturn, occupying Virgo, with its ruler Mercury. In effect, there's a Saturn/Mercury connection. This interpretation process is similar to the analysis of a two-planet conjunction. Saturn represents focus and Mercury represents the mind, resulting in an interpretation stating a "focused mind" if the planets are positive, or a "stuck mind" if the planets are negative. Additionally, we know that Virgo is the sixth sign of the zodiac, so Saturn in Mercury's sign will also be colored by Virgo's sixth house traits. That could generate a mind focused on service, if positive, or a health problem with obsessive/compulsive behavior, if negative.

A planet won't always occupy the same sign that it rules because they're constantly in motion. It's considered strong when a planet is found, at a specific time and location in its celestial travels, in its own sign. All planets, except for the Sun and Moon, are assigned to rule two signs. Some authors differ as to what signs, if any, are ruled by Rahu and Ketu. The degrees indicate the position within a sign that gives the planet a strong influence.

Own Sign: A planet that occupies the same sign that it rules is said to be in its own sign, or "at home," and will enjoy the benefits that anyone would have living within their own domain.

Exaltation: This is one of the strongest positions for a planet in the chart. It brings strong effects to the planet, if not modified by unfavorable aspects (such as residing in a negative placement or sitting along with malefic planets).

Debilitation: This is one of the weakest places for a planet to occupy. The planet can't fully release its positive traits, and malefic planets become worse. The planet can't defend itself well.

Moolatrikona: Gives favorable results to planets, and makes unfavorable planets less negative. This position is stronger than own sign, but not as strong as exaltation, which is the strongest.

Sandhi: A planet becomes weaker when it's located at the beginning of a sign and is under one degree, or when it's at the end of a sign or 29 degrees or more.

Combust: A planet is said to lose its power when it's very close in degrees to the Sun. While this effect does exist, the chart reader should be careful to note that Mercury and Venus are often close to the Sun, and the effect of this might not be as disastrous as some astrologers state. For instance, many important planetary yogas involve conjunctions with the Sun.

Retrograde: There is debate among scholars concerning the effect of retrograde planets. It's said that a retrograde planet becomes stronger, but this doesn't mean it will necessarily be more favorable. All the effects on a planet must be taken into consideration when looking at the retrograde effect. Many astrologers feel that planets, such as the sensitive Mercury, aren't favorable when retrograde, and more or less reverse the good influence of the planet.

The following section lists the traits and inclinations of each planet along with some of the myths associated with each Vedic planet.

The Sun
Surya or Ravi (soo' ree yah; rah' vee)

How We Act and Direct

Surya or Ravi: A traditional Vedic image of the deity of the Sun.

Common Abbreviation: Su

Key Words: Father; activity; leading; ego; vitality; personal power

Zodiac Ruler of: Leo

Favorable Traits: Directs and inspires others; thinks big; positive; self-confident; generous

Unfavorable Traits: Pompous; vain; arrogant; power hungry

Chart Significator for: 1st house (body, health, and personal self); 9th house (father); 10th house (career, status or reputation, life purpose)

Carries Its Influence to: Leo rising; the 5th house; Sun in 1st

Best Direction: East

Best Day: Sunday

Energizing Color: Copper or orange-red; gold

Energy/Gender: Masculine

Guna/Temperament: Sattva (pure)

Caste: Kshatriya (warrior)

Ayurvedic Constitution: Pitta (fire)

Planetary Cabinet: King (leader)

Motion: The Sun stays for one month in each sign, and it takes one year to travel through the zodiac.

Governing Deity: *Agni,* "The God of Fire" (according to Parashara); *Surya Narayana* (nah rah' yah na) (according to common use)

Planetary Friendships: Friendly to the Moon, Mars, and Jupiter; an enemy to Venus and Saturn; neutral to Mercury

Sun Mythology—Description of Sun according to Parashara: The Sun's eyes are honey-colored and he has a square body. He is of clean habits, pitta, intelligent, and has limited hair (on his head).

Sun Mythology—General Description: Surya or Ravi, the Sun god, is a royal deity and king of all the planets. The Sun god has two arms, each holding a lotus. He's called "The Awakener of the Lotus"—the lotus being the flower and symbol of the mind opening up and becoming enlightened. Sometimes Surya is shown as a form of Vishnu, called Surya Narayana, where his four arms hold the traditional conch, discus, loop, and hook. He's seated in a chariot drawn by seven horses, sometimes represented as the seven meters of the Vedas. This chariot only has one wheel but is built with 12 spokes, symbolizing the 12 months and the wheel or circle of the zodiac.

Surya is sometimes shown standing on a pedestal or seated in a lotus. The Sun represents Brahma, who arose from a shining celestial egg, chanting "Om"—the first sound of creation. The sound, called *Shabda Brahman,* initiated the process of creation. It also triggered the start of the rishi's cognition of the Vedas. (It's interesting that the Western Bible states: "In the beginning was the Word.") Brahma appeared under his name of *Ka* or *Hiranyagharba,* manifesting and sustaining the world. This image of the Sun, in its form as the shining golden center of the world, looks somewhat like astronomy photos we see today of the radiant cluster of stars at the center of our Milky Way galaxy.

A traditional Vedic image of the Moon.

The Moon
Chandra or Soma (chahn' drah; so' mah)

How We Feel and Respond

Your Moon Sign

The Moon plays a significant role in Vedic astrology analysis. Because of this, the sign in which your Moon is placed in the birth chart is traditionally called your *janma rasi* (jahn' mah rah' shee), or "birth sign." The star or nakshatra in which your Moon is placed is called your *janma nakshatra,* or "birth star." A Vedic priest will ask for your birth star if you ever participate in certain Vedic rituals, such as *pujas* (poo' jahs), *yagyas* (yahg' yahs), and *homas* (hoh' mahs), or "fire sacrifices."

Common Abbreviation: Mo

Key Words: Mother; nourishing; supportive; emotional

Zodiac Ruler of: Cancer

Favorable Traits: Motherly; intuitive; instinctual; social; humanitarian; imaginative

Unfavorable Traits: Cares too much; doesn't know how to disengage; victim; emotional hypersensitivity

Chart Significator for: 4th house (mother, emotions, home)

Carries Its Influence to: Cancer rising; Moon in 1st; 4th house

Best Direction: Northwest

Best Day: Monday

Energizing Color: White

Energy/Gender: Feminine

Guna/Temperament: Sattva (pure)

Caste: Vaishya (merchant)

Ayurvedic Constitution: Kapha (water/earth), but can also be vata (airy)

Planetary Cabinet: Queen

Motion: Takes approximately 2.5 days to travel through a sign

Governing Deity: *Varuna* (according to Parashara); *Uma* (oo' mah) or *Parvati* (pahr' vah tee) (by common use)

Planetary Friendships: Friends with the Sun and Mercury; neutral to Mars, Jupiter, Venus, and Saturn; Moon doesn't consider any planet its enemy (however, Saturn, Mercury, Venus, and Rahu and Ketu consider the Moon to be their enemy)

Moon Mythology—Description of Moon according to Parashara: The Moon is very vata and kapha. She is learned and has a round body. She has auspicious looks and sweet speech, is fickle-minded, and very lustful.

Moon Mythology—General Description: Moon, or *Chandra,* also called *Soma,* is considered to be about 70 years old and a royal planet representing the queen. It's also the *Matru karaka* (mah' troo kahr' ah kah), or the significator for the Mother. The Moon god is shown with a fair complexion and white garments, traveling on a lotus pedestal in a white chariot pulled by seven white horses. The Moon holds a mace in one hand while the other hand is raised in a gesture of blessing. Sometimes the Moon is also depicted holding a white lotus in each hand. While all the grahas, or planets, are considered male, some planets, such as the Moon, carry feminine significations or characteristics. As in the case of the Moon, we see motherhood, fertility, gestation, feminine energy and the like.

The Moon was the son of Maharishi Atri and married the 27 daughters of Daksha Prajapati, who were in essence the 27 nakshatras (Moon signs) of astrology. The Moon visited each of his wives for one day a month, but showed more favor to Rohini nakshatra. At another point, Soma has a dalliance with Tara, the wife of Brihaspati, the guru of all the devas. He took her to Shukracharya's (Venus's) ashram, where all the asuras (demons) resided. Shukra counseled

Soma, telling him that his deed was inappropriate, to which Soma came to his senses and returned Tara to her home. While Brihaspati forgave Soma for his indiscretion, Soma's father-in-law, Daksha, cursed the Moon with consumption for doing this, which caused the Moon to slowly decay in brightness each month. Chandra's intimacy with Brihaspati's wife led to the birth of the planet Mercury.

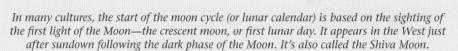

In many cultures, the start of the moon cycle (or lunar calendar) is based on the sighting of the first light of the Moon—the crescent moon, or first lunar day. It appears in the West just after sundown following the dark phase of the Moon. It's also called the Shiva Moon.

Astronomy of the Moon

Vedic astrologers developed a method to track the daily motion of the Moon. This is referred to as a *tithi* (tih' tee), which translates as "lunar day." The tithi is a measure of the phase of the Moon, which is also a measure of the difference in longitude between the Sun and the Moon. There are 15 tithis assigned to the bright half of the lunar month *(shukla paksha)*, when the Moon is waxing—that is, going from New to Full—and 15 tithis assigned to the dark half of the lunar month *(krishna paksha)*, when the moon is going from Full to New, or waning.

The lunar days add up to a lunar month. There are a couple ways of categorizing this month. One is called *synodic*, or the time it takes to go from New Moon *(amavasa)* to the next New Moon, or Full Moon *(poornima)* to the next Full Moon in some calendar systems. Another type of lunar month is the sidereal lunar month. This is the time it takes the Moon to start and return to the same location in reference to a marker star. This period of Moon time is about 27.32 days, making it closer to 27 than 28. It takes about 29.5 days for the Moon to go from one new Moon to the next.

It's easier to use the new Moon to tell the start of the month because the sliver of the Moon appears as the first light after the darkness of the new Moon. Also, it's hard to tell when the Moon is completely full, if that were to be used as the starting point of the lunar month.

Mangala, also known as Kuja (koo' jah), Angaraka (angh' ah kah), Keya Karttikeya (kahr' tuh kay yah), Skanda (skhan' dah), and Murugan (moo' roo gahn)— a traditional Vedic image of Mars.

Mars
Mangala or Kuja (muhn' gah lah, koo' jah)

How We Execute and Take Action

Common Abbreviation: Ma

Keywords: Siblings; action; energy; fighting; guarding; self-directed

Zodiac Ruler of: Aries and Scorpio

Favorable Traits: Executive qualities; courageous; competitive; freedom fighter

Unfavorable Traits: Impulsive; angry; self-seeking; combative; thief

Chart Significator for: 3rd house (younger siblings, courage and determination, communication, courage); 6th house (warriors, enemies and opposition, diseases, accidents, and injuries)

Carries Its Influence to: Aries or Scorpio rising; Mars in 1st; 8th house

Best Direction: South

Best Day: Tuesday

Energizing Color: Red

Energy/Gender: Masculine

Guna/Temperament: Tamas (destructive quality—which can serve positive purposes)

Caste: Kshatriya (warrior)

Ayurvedic Constitution: Pitta (fire)

Planetary Cabinet: Military Commander

Motion: Mars takes about 45 days (or six weeks) to travel through one zodiac sign

Governing Deity: *Subramaniya* (soo' brah mah' nee yah), Shiva's son (according to Parashara); Shiva (according to common usage)

Planetary Friendships: Mars is friends with the Sun, Moon, and Jupiter; enemy of Mercury; neutral to Venus and Saturn

Mars Mythology—Description of Mars according to Parashara: Mars is cruel, has blood-red eyes, is fickle-minded, liberal, pitta (fire), given to anger, and has a narrow waist and thin physique.

Mars Mythology—General Description: Mars is considered to be about 16 years old. He has four arms, holding a mace, trident, and other war weapons. He has red hair and his hairy body is also reddish (after *Rudra,* the image of Shiva as "ruddy" and "roaring"). His vehicle is a ram and he wears red garments.

Mars is regarded as *Bhumiputra* or *Kuja,* the Son of the Earth. At one point in creation, the planet Earth was submerged in the celestial waters. Vishnu came and lifted the earth out of the water, placing it in its orbit. Mother Earth was most grateful for this and offered to bear a child for Vishnu. He agreed, and out of their union came the planet Mars, or Kuja. A variation on this myth states that Mars was the result of the union of Shiva and Mother Earth. Mars is also called *Angaraka,* or "Burning Coal." Some people are fearful of Mars's fierce effects and try to appease him by calling him *Mangala,* "The Auspicious One."

A traditional Vedic image of Mercury.

Mercury

Budha (boo' dah)

How We Think and Speak

Common Abbreviation: Me

Key Words: Cousins; communicating; thinking; writing; calculating; speaking

Zodiac Ruler of: Gemini and Virgo

Favorable Traits: Discriminating (in the positive sense); communicative (speaking and writing); scientific capacity; inventive; versatile; humorous

Unfavorable Traits: Nervous; conflicted; talks too much; critical; sarcastic

Chart Significator for: 3rd house (communication, writing); 5th house (intellect, spiritual techniques, business); 10th house (career)

Carries Its Influence to: Gemini or Virgo rising; Mercury in 1st; 3rd and 6th houses

Best Direction: North

Best Day: Wednesday

Energizing Color: Green

Energy/Gender: Neutral (neither masculine nor feminine)

Guna/Temperament: Rajas (active)

Caste: Vaishya (merchant)

Ayurvedic Constitution: Vata (air)

Planetary Cabinet: Prince (some also say messenger or scribe)

Motion: Takes about a month to traverse a sign; in an astrological chart, Mercury never gets more than 27 degrees away from the Sun

Governing Deity: Maha Vishnu (according to Parashara); Saraswati, the Goddess of Music and Learning (in common usage)

Planetary Friendships: Mercury is friendly to the Sun and Venus; enemy to the Moon; neutral to Mars, Jupiter, Saturn, Rahu, and Ketu

Mercury Mythology—Description of Mercury according to Parashara: Mercury is endowed with an attractive physique and the capacity to make puns and use words with double meaning. He has a sense of humor and is fond of jokes. He has a mix of all three ayurvedic doshas, or body types.

Mercury Mythology—General Description: Mercury is considered to be about 20 years old. In Mercury's four arms, he carries a sword, a shield, and a mace or club, with the fourth hand held in a gesture of blessing. He wears green garments and his vehicle is a lion. He rides in a white chariot illuminated by light and drawn by ten horses who are as fast as the wind, and as fast as thought.

Mercury's father is Soma, the Moon. His mother is Tara, the wife of Brihaspati, the Guru of the Gods. He was given the name *Budha,* which means "intelligent" or "wise," by the creator Brahma because of his quick mind. He's

knowledgeable in all the Vedic scriptures. Brahma made Mercury the lord
of the Earth and gave him the status
of a planet. He's generally considered
auspicious but sensitive, and if disturbed
he can trigger natural disasters such as
droughts, floods, and according to some,
earthquakes.

JUPITER
Guru or Brihaspati (goo' roo, bree hus' puh tee)

How We Know and Grow

Brihaspati or Guru, a traditional Vedic image of Jupiter.

Common Abbreviation: Ju

Key Words: Wisdom; growth; knowledge; education; prosperity

Zodiac Ruler of: Sagittarius and Pisces

Favorable Traits: Wisdom; justice; counseling; optimism; caring; plays fair

Unfavorable Traits: Overindulgent; too leisurely; extravagant; overestimates

Chart Significator for: 2nd house (accumulated wealth and liquid assets); 5th house (intellect, *shastras* or "teachings," spiritual techniques); 9th house (God, guru, counselors, teachers, fortune, right behavior); 11th house (opportunities and gains, cash flow, older siblings, friends, and influential people)

Carries Its Influence to: Sagittarius or Pisces rising: Jupiter in 1st; 9th and 12th houses

Best Direction: Northeast

Best Day: Thursday

Energizing Color: Gold or yellow

Energy/Gender: Male

Guna/Temperament: Sattva (pure)

Caste: Brahmin (priest, teacher, or guru)

Ayurvedic Constitution: Kapha (water/earth)

Planetary Cabinet: Minister/counselor/advisor

Motion: Jupiter remains in each zodiac sign for about a year

Governing Deity: Indra, the Chief of the Gods (according to Parashara); also *Dakshina Murthi*, or "Shiva as the Teacher" and Brihaspati, Guru of the Gods (according to common usage)

Planetary Friendships: Jupiter is friends with the Sun, Moon, and Mars; Mercury and Venus are his enemies (yet no planet considers the benevolent Jupiter their enemy); he is neutral with Saturn; friendly to Rahu but neutral to Ketu

Jupiter Mythology—Description of Jupiter according to Parashara: Jupiter has a big body, tawny hair and eyes, is kapha, intelligent, and learned in shastras.

Jupiter Mythology—General Description: Jupiter (called Guru or Brihaspati), "The Lord of Prayers," is also known as the *Gurudeva*, or the "Guru of the Gods." He holds a stick *(danda)*, holy *Rudraksha* beads, and a small pot in three of his hands. His fourth hand is raised in a gesture of blessing.

Jupiter rides in a golden chariot drawn by eight golden horses who are as fast as the wind. His weapon is a golden staff. He has a golden complexion and is dressed in yellow garments. He's often shown seated on a lotus flower. Jupiter is the son of Maharishi Angirasa, whose wife performed a special vow with great

devotion to the Sanat Kumars (Ashwinis).
They granted her a boon of a very wise
son who would know all the shastras, or
Vedic scriptures. One story tells us that
the asuras were attempting to weaken the
devas by obstructing the offerings from a
yagya (sacrificial ritual) being performed
for them. Jupiter used a special mantra
and drove off the asuras, allowing the
devas to nourish themselves with the
ritual offerings. In order to become the
guru of the devas, Jupiter did a special
tapas (penance) to Lord Shiva. Shiva was
pleased with Jupiter's dedication and
granted him the privilege of being the
"Guru to the Gods."

A traditional Vedic image of Venus.

Venus
Shukra (shoo' krah)

How We Love, Enjoy, and Relate

Common Abbreviation: Ve

Key Words: Relating; loving; the partner; the middle man; beauty and art

Zodiac Ruler of: Taurus and Libra

Favorable Traits: Mannerly; social skills; artistic sense; helps others achieve balance and rapport

Unfavorable Traits: Indulgent and pleasure-seeking; unproductive; manipulator for their needs; romance clouds vision

Chart Significator for: 4th house (vehicles, comforts); 7th house (spouse, wife, relationships in general, contracts)

Carries Its Influence to: Taurus or Libra rising; Venus in the 1st; 2nd and 7th houses

Direction: Southeast

Best Day: Friday

Energizing Color: White or silver-white

Energy/Gender: Feminine (yet all graha deities are male in form)

Guna/Temperament: Rajas (active)

Caste: Brahmin

Ayurvedic Constitution: Kapha (water); sometimes vata (air)

Planetary Cabinet: Counselor/advisor/mediator

Motion: Venus spends about a month in each sign of the zodiac; Venus never travels more than 48 degrees from the Sun.

Governing Deity: Indrani, or Sachi Devi, the wife of Indra; also Maha Lakshmi (according to common usage)

Planetary Friendships: Venus is friends with Mercury and Saturn; enemy of the Sun, Moon, and Mars; neutral to Jupiter.

Venus Mythology—Description of Venus according to Parashara: Venus is charming, has a splendorous physique, is excellent or great in disposition, has beautiful and bright eyes, is a poet, is kapha and vata, and has curly hair.

Venus Mythology—General Description: While Jupiter is the *Shukracharya*, "Guru of the Gods," Venus is the *Daityaguru* (die' tyah goo' roo), or "Guru of the Asuras (demons)." He's the son of the sage Brighu and is represented as very youthful—some say as young as seven. Venus rides a white chariot adorned by flags and pulled by eight fiery horses. He is of white complexion and he holds a danda (stick), holy *Rudraksha* beads, and a small pot in three of his hands. His fourth hand is raised in a gesture of blessing.

Venus performed a severe tapas (penance) to Lord Shiva, and being pleased, Shiva granted Venus a special knowledge called *Mritasanjivani* (mree' tah sahn' jee vah nee), which enabled him to raise people from the dead. Shiva also made Venus incapable of being killed and granted him the role of "Lord of Wealth." He's a master of herbs and mantras and is skilled in generating all kinds of tastes. In his role as guru to the asuras, he resuscitated the asuras after they'd been killed in battle with the devas. Venus eventually gave all his wealth to the asuras and retired as a recluse. Brahma also conferred upon him the position of a planet. One of his skills as a planet is to pacify the other planets who might cause an obstruction to rain, an essential part of India's monsoon-based agriculture.

Saturn
Shani (shaw' nee)

How We Focus, Take Responsibility,
and Regulate Our Lives

Common Abbreviation: Sa

Key Words: Focus; order; structure; regulation;
conservation; control; discipline; time

Zodiac Ruler of: Capricorn and Aquarius

Favorable Traits: Dependable; persevering; orderly;
structured

Unfavorable Traits: Morose; boring; works too hard;
cruel; doesn't have enough fun; poor; restricted

Chart Significator for: 8th house (longevity, death,
chronic illnesses); 12th house (losses, places of solitude,
moksha, spiritual detachment)

Carries Its Influence to: Capricorn or Aquarius rising;
Saturn in 1st; 11th or 12th houses

Best Direction: West

*Shani—
a traditional
Vedic image
of Saturn.*

Best Day: Saturday

Energizing Color: Dark blue or black

Energy/Gender: Neutral (neither masculine nor feminine)

Guna/Temperament: Tamas (inertia)

Caste: Sudra (servant)

Ayurvedic Constitution: Vata (air)

Planetary Cabinet: Servant/service provider

Motion: Saturn is the slowest moving planet—it takes approximately 2.5 years to transit a sign, and it completes a circuit of the zodiac in 30 years.

Governing Deity: Brahma (according to Parashara); Yama (yah' mah) the Lord of Death and Shiva are sometimes associated with Saturn according to common usage.

Planetary Friendships: Saturn is friendly to Mercury and Venus; enemies are the Sun, Moon, and Mars; neutral to Jupiter; Rahu and Ketu are counted among his friends.

Saturn Mythology—Description of Saturn according to Parashara: Saturn has an emaciated and long physique, tawny eyes, big teeth, and is vata in temperament. He's indolent, lame, and has coarse hair.

Saturn Mythology—General Description: Saturn is very slow and old—some say around 100 years. His name, *Shani*, means "slow-moving." He carries a bow and arrow, a trident, and a thin rod in three of his hands, and his fourth hand is represented giving a gesture of blessing. He's shown mounted on a vulture, black crow, or water buffalo. Saturn's chariot is made of iron. Although dark, he's the son of Surya (the Sun god) and Chaya (Shadow).

While some associate Saturn with misfortune, he's had some of that himself. His mother kicked him in a fit of rage, leaving him lame. The Divine Mother, Parvati, cursed Saturn, but felt regretful afterward and granted a boon that no important work would succeed unless Saturn was given his proper due—especially when he was transiting or aspecting at the time of that event.

Saturn assumes the role of Yama, and as such is looked upon as a factor in the end of life. Saturn also represents detachment and has great value in sustaining a spiritual life. No *sanyasi* (monk) can persist in that role unless they have a well-placed Saturn in their birth chart (and a weak Venus).

Myth of the Celestial Snakes, Soma, and the Moon

The great celestial ocean was being churned at one time in the past in order to remove the poison in it and to filter out the celestial ambrosia, called Soma or *amrita* (anti-death)—the drink of immortality. Vishnu didn't want the asuras (demons) to become empowered by drinking this vitalizing potion, so they weren't allowed in line to drink of the Soma. However, a clever asura called *Swarbhanu* (swar bah' noo) created confusion amongst the deities by asking them who should be first in line to drink the Soma. In the debate and distraction that followed, the asura cut in line and took a drink of the Soma. The Sun and Moon saw this and alerted Vishnu, who threw his disk (the *Sudarshana Chakra*) at the asura, severing its head. However, since it had already taken a drink, the demon was now immortal, although now sitting in two pieces.

Since the demon had attained a form of divinity, Brahma made him into a planet and allowed him to sit in his assembly with the other planets. His severed head was named *Rahu,* and his tail was named *Ketu.* Rahu and Ketu have never forgiven the Sun and Moon for alerting Vishnu about their Soma drinking, so they continue to harass them by creating eclipses. As such, the demon is called *Rahu Parag* (pah' rahg).

The 108 demons and asuras pull the serpent Vasuki back and forth around the pole of Mount Meru, churning the celestial ocean to extract the invigorating Soma, the nectar of the gods.

North Node of the Moon
Rahu (rah' hoo)

To Unveil or to Shadow

Note: Rahu, as a node, is created as the shadow of something else. Its identity is in its associations, so chart significations and where it carries its influence will depend on its location and association with other planets.

Common Abbreviation: Ra

Key Words: Material purpose; acquisition; to continue; uncovering; masking or obscuring; foreign; purifying or toxifying

Zodiac Ruler of: No ruler is specifically stated in most Vedic texts

Favorable Traits: Innovative; adapts in foreign environments; material success; investigative

Unfavorable Traits: Toxic; deceptive; treacherous; confused; loses by not paying attention

Chart Significator for: 8th house (also see preceding note)

A traditional Vedic image of the North Node of the Moon.

Carries Its Influence to: Said to act like Saturn (see note); Capricorn and Aquarius (Saturn-owned signs)

Best Direction: Southwest

Best Day: Saturday (said to take on features of Saturn)

Best Color: Medium honey-red or rusty red-orange

Energy/Gender: Masculine

Guna/Temperament: Takes on characteristic of planets associated with it; can be tamas, since it deals with poisons and shadows

Caste: Takes on characteristic of planets associated with it; can be sudra (servant)

Ayurvedic Constitution: Vata (airy); acts like Saturn

Planetary Cabinet: Army personnel, especially secret services

Motion: Rahu takes about 18 months to transit one sign of the zodiac

Governing Deity: Parashara doesn't name a deity for Rahu, but many assign Durga as the deity.

Planetary Friendships: Rahu is friendly toward Jupiter, Venus, and Saturn; considers Sun and Moon as its enemy; neutral to Mercury.

Rahu Mythology—Description of Rahu according to Parashara: Rahu has a smoky appearance with a blue mixed physique. He resides in forests and is horrible. He is vata in temperament and is intelligent.

Rahu Mythology—General Description: Rahu is dressed in black clothes. He holds a sword, a shield, and a trident in each of his three hands, respectively. His fourth hand is raised in a gesture of blessing. He sits on a lion. Rahu's chariot, which is pulled by eight black horses, is represented as a form of darkness itself. Rahu is considered the deity of the shadow (chaya) of the Earth. He covers the Earth with this shadow during eclipses to such a degree that people on Earth get confused by the darkness he creates. While Rahu has no "body" like the other planets, and is the point where the Sun and Moon's orbits cross each other, Rahu can be seen by the shadow he creates.

The Moon passes in front, eclipsing the light of the Sun.

Ketu, a traditional Vedic image of the South Node of the Moon.

South Node of the Moon
Ketu (keh' too)

To Reorganize and Enlighten

Note: Ketu, as a node, is created as the shadow of something else. Its identity is in its associations, so chart significations and where it carries its influence to will depend on its location and association with other planets.

Common Abbreviation: Ke

Key Words: Spiritual purpose; transcendence; unboundedness; discontinuity; reorganization; hypersensitivity; surprises

Zodiac Ruler of: No ruler is specifically stated in most Vedic texts

Favorable Traits: Highly adaptable; very intuitive; spiritual nature; helps reorganize others

Unfavorable Traits: Chaotic; ungrounded; doesn't finish; unstable; undependable

Chart Significator for: 12th house *(moksha bhava)*

Carries Its Influence to: Said to act like Mars, Scorpio, and

8th house (see preceding note)

Best Direction: Heavenward (no specific direction or all directions)

Best Day: Tuesday (said to take on features of Mars); some say Friday because Ketu is associated with the deity Ganesh

Energizing Color: Multicolored and striped items

Energy/Gender: Masculine; sometimes sexless

Guna/Temperament: Takes on characteristic of planets associated with it; can be rajas because of changeability or sattva because of spiritual orientation

Caste: Takes on characteristic of planets associated with it; can be Brahmin-like since it's a spiritual seeker

Planetary Cabinet: None

Ayurvedic Constitution: Pitta (fire); acts like Mars; changeable nature of Ketu can make it act in a vata mode as well

Motion: Ketu is always in the opposite sign to Rahu and moves at the same speed of about 18 months in a sign of the zodiac

Governing Deity: Parashara doesn't name a deity, but many associate Ketu with Ganesh, the elephant God, in his role of *Ganapati*, the "Remover of Obstacles."

Planetary Friendships: Ketu is friends with Mars, Venus, and Saturn; it considers Sun and Moon as his enemies; is neutral to Mercury and Jupiter.

Ketu Mythology—Description of Ketu according to Parashara: Ketu is akin to Rahu.

Ketu Mythology—General Description: Ketu is shown with two arms, one holding a mace while the other gives a gesture of blessing. Technically, he is the headless body of Rahu, but is shown with a head out of respect. Ketu is represented by comets and by waving flags.

Ketu wears either multicolored, striped, or black clothes. His body is smoky and his face is often depicted as disfigured or diseased in some way (missing, actually!). He rides upon a vulture. As with Rahu, his counterpart, he was conferred the title of planet by Brahma after he was made immortal from drinking the Soma juice.

Ganesh seated with his adoring mouse, Mushika.

Budha, planet Mercury.

CHAPTER FOUR

BHA CHAKRA: THE VEDIC ZODIAC

The Kundalini [the horoscope diagram] *is a Power. This Power contains in it the planets created by Vishnu, moving in the 12-segmented zodiac.*
— Varahamihira

Now that you have an understanding of the planets, our next step is to determine how to find the planets in relationship to the sky. We'll look from the geocentric point of view of our rotating and revolving location on Earth. On a dark, moonless night, you can probably see around 1,500 stars without a telescope. They all look pretty much the same—some brighter than others, but basically just tiny luminous dots on the black backdrop of night. To help remember them, as well as locate them, the ancient sky observers gave these little stargroups names and attached pictures and stories to them. (Over the generations, the heart can remember more through stories than the mind can retain through formula.) Forming mythological star groups with special stories gave the astronomer/priests a common way to identify and connect the dots of the stars, as well as a standard way to describe them to others. It told those who were using their star charts what they were looking at. These charts became even more useful as a way to accurately show the positions of the stars in smaller regions of space and to indicate which planets were passing through them at any time of the day, month, and year—thus, the foundations of the birth chart and the zodiac.

The zodiac, invented by the early astronomer/astrologers, is a circular band of 12 constellations, or star groups, that lie in the plane of the solar system. The Greeks called it the *zodiac,* or "band of animals." The Vedic rishis saw it as a starry path reminding them of a chakra, or wheel. They called it the *bhachakra,* meaning "circle of stars." It was a cosmic mandala looking like the *Sudarshana Chakra,* the discus of the universal MahaVishnu, swirling around his up-pointed finger. The swirling disk can also be seen in the pattern of a spiral galaxy, such as our Milky Way.

The planets pass through these 12 sections on a center line drawn out by the 360-degree apparent circle of the Sun. The wheel of the zodiac traces out the pathway of the planets approximately 8 to 9 degrees north and south (above and below) the apparent journey of the Sun around the Earth. The longitudinal (East/West) location of the planets is measured along the ecliptic in degrees, minutes, and seconds of arc. This measurement of longitude along the ecliptic is what astrology tracks in terms of twelve 30-degree sections or signs. Vedic Astrology generally doesn't measure distance of planets above or below the ecliptic line, although some astrologers do track it.

The signs of the zodiac provide a framework to observe and record the interaction of planets. You can see this band of stars and the planets traversing them and observe the arc they make just looking south above the horizon line at night. The zodiac belt is a useful tool for observations made from a location on the surface of the Earth because a shining object in the night sky can't be a planet if it doesn't lie within the band of the zodiac. (Also, stars shimmer in their light and planets don't.) It's important to note that the zodiac signs are 30-degree sections of the sky in terms of space, not time. The houses, which we'll discuss later, give us the ability to track the position of planets in terms of one's local time.

The astronomers of old also observed that eclipses occurred along this starry corridor, so this pathway of the planets was called the *ecliptic*. Surya, the Sun, was represented as riding on a flaming chariot, driven by Aruna, the rosy dawn. His celestial car had one wheel and 12 spokes. Thus we get the imagery of the ecliptic and the 12 divisions of the zodiac, as originally described several thousand years ago.

LOCATING THE SUN IN THE CONSTELLATIONS

The observational astronomers kept track of the stars at night and extrapolated where the Sun would be in relationship to the stars during the days ahead. The astronomers figured out which sign the Sun occupied by observing which zodiac constellation was the last to rise before the Sun came up, or which was the first constellation to set after the Sun set. Calendars were created from this knowledge.

Most people are aware that astrologers, especially those of the West, determine your Sun sign by marking the position of the Sun in the zodiac on the day and month of your birth. This is made even more specific by noting your location—that is, the city, state, and country where you were born. So if the Sun was in Taurus on the date of your birth, it means the constellation of Taurus was behind the Sun at that time. You would have to wait about half a year for the Earth to revolve to the other side of the Sun to actually see that constellation during the night.

It's good to remember, however, that Vedic astrology calculates the position of the Sun, Moon, and all the planets—not just the sign occupied by the Sun—and regards the Lagna (rising sign) and the Moon as more significant than the Sun in many ways.

STARTING THE CIRCLE OF THE CYCLES

Since astrology deals with cycles of nature, the geometry of a circle plays

a major role in this Science of Time and Space. As we've learned, the circle of the Sun around the Earth, with its daily rising and setting and its larger circle through all the zodiac constellations, forms the primary circle of astrology—the band of the zodiac. As is the case with all circles and cycles, we have to ask, "Where does the circle of the zodiac start in terms of space and time?"

There are two major zodiacs in the world of astrology: (1) a zodiac of signs, also called *tropical,* and (2) a zodiac of stars or constellations, also referred to as *sidereal.* Each of these

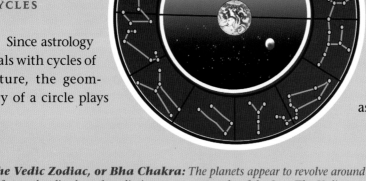

The Vedic Zodiac, or Bha Chakra: *The planets appear to revolve around the Earth through a band of stars that lie along the ecliptic, or apparent path, of the Sun. The Vedic system shows the entrance of the Sun into the sign of Aries around April 14—not around March 21 as is the tropical convention. This 24-day or 24-degree difference is called the Ayanamsa, and is caused by precession.*

zodiacs divides the ecliptic or path of the Sun into the same 12 segments, from Aries through Pisces. After the naming of the zodiac segments, the differences between the two systems start to emerge.

Western astrologers work with a zodiac of signs, related to seasons (tropical). The tropical signs are defined by the equinoxes and the tropical (turning) points of the solstices, most specifically the vernal equinox, which marks the start of the sign of Aries around March 21 each year.

Vedic astrology has chosen to keep the astrological *signs* of the zodiac fixed as close as possible to the stars that bear their name, thus it's called *sidereal* or "star based." The start of the sidereal zodiac is based on that point when the Sun enters the constellation of Aries, around April 14 each year. The Vedic system uses a marker star to define the start of the sign/constellation of Aries. The most popular marker star, defined by the government of India, was developed by L. C. Lahiri, and is called *Lahiri Ayanamsa* or *Chitra Paksha* (chih' trah pahk' shah) *Ayanamsa*. This starting point of Aries is identified by the passage of the Sun at a point 180 degrees opposite the star Alpha Virginis, and the main star of the nakshatra of Chitra (we'll discuss nakshatras in more detail in the next chapter). Since the stars are obscured by the light of the Sun during the day, it's the convention to pick a star at night, or at dawn in the West, and measure 180 degrees opposite that to identify the point where the Sun enters Aries.

ALIGNMENT OF SIGNS TO CONSTELLATIONS

While the Vedic system attempts to keep the signs in alignment with the stars, this alignment isn't exact. It's as precise as can be in matching the randomly configured constellations in the heavens to the dozen 30-degree, evenly spaced zodiac signs. Some star groups extend beyond the limits of the 12 zodiac signs, and some fall well within these 30-degree segments of the sky.

The following list gives the approximate length, in degrees, of each of the star groups or constellations of the zodiac, as defined in 1930 by the International Astronomical Union (IAU):

- Aries (24°)
- Taurus (36°)
- Gemini (28°)
- Cancer (21°)

- Leo (35°)
- Virgo (46°)
- Libra (18°)
- Scorpio (31°)

- Sagittarius (30°)
- Capricorn (28°)
- Aquarius (25°)
- Pisces (38°)

PRECESSION AND AYANAMSA

Originally, the stars or constellations were fairly close to their namesakes of the 12 zodiac signs. At one time, around A.D. 285, at the vernal (spring) equinox, we could see that the Sun rose in the constellation or stars of Aries as well as within the created boundaries of the zodiac sign of Aries. This was due to the fact that the Earth wobbles backward on its axis about one degree every 72 years. This causes the orientation of the signs to slip backward with respect to the constellations.

Today, when the Sun rises at the vernal equinox, around March 21, it ascends with the stars of the constellation of Pisces in the background, not Aries. In fact, since the first millennium, the slip has rendered a precession of about 24 degrees, meaning in fact that the vernal equinox is occurring at six degrees of the sidereal sign of Pisces now. We're now experiencing the "dawning of the age of Aquarius," which should take over with the Sun rising in the constellation of Aquarius at the spring equinox around A.D. 2437, give or take a few years. (Some say this event will occur closer to A.D. 2600—it depends on where you mark the starting alignment of the sign and constellation of Aries and what you consider to be the boundary marker for Aquarius.)

As I've mentioned, tropical astrology bases the marking of the first degree of the sign Aries on the start of the spring season, even though the stars behind the Sun at that time are, again, those of the constellation of Pisces. The approximate 24-degree or 24-day difference from where the two systems mark the first degree of Aries (March 21 vs. April 14) is called the *Ayanamsa* (ayan am' shah).

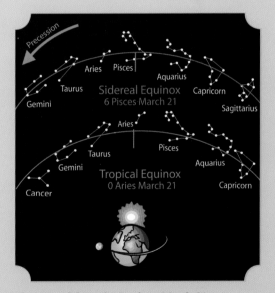

Another view of precession: *Looking up and eastward from the Earth on March 21, you'll see that the Sun actually rises in stars (sidereal) of the constellation of Pisces, very close to the constellation of Aquarius. It's about 24 degrees short of Aries on the equinox.*

Ancient cultures often depicted the demons (negative beings) pulling the stars backwards or anticlockwise in the sky, i.e. precession. The devas (positive beings) were shown pulling to maintain the rotation of the skies in the natural clockwise manner. Some cultures viewed precession as "the sky is falling!"

For a quick conversion from tropical to sidereal, you can subtract 24 degrees from your tropical planetary positions and get an approximate sidereal position of planets. As I stated earlier in noting the differences between Western and Vedic astrology, in most cases, your tropical Sun sign will move back by a sign—unless you were born around the 15th to 20th of the month, whereby the Sun will stay in the same sign.

VEDIC CHART FORMATS

The natal chart is a diagram, like a photo take by a camera with a built-in time and date stamp. The chart is a snapshot of the positions of stars and planets relative to a point and time on Earth. If we take a picture of the heavens from a different place on Earth, at a different time, the stars in the photo will be different. Because of the uniqueness of the rotation of the Earth, its revolution around the Sun, and the solar system's journey around the center of our Milky Way galaxy, this exact point in time and space will not be repeated for about 26,000 years! While we're all the same in some way, there's always something unique that differentiates us as humans. The chart reflects that.

The format of the Vedic horoscope takes different shapes according to whether one follows the convention of North or South India. As you will see, these charts are square, unlike the modern round Western charts. It's interesting to note that medieval European astrologers used a chart format similar to the northern India style.

It's also important to note that the horoscope chart (the word *horoscope* comes from the Greek for "hour watcher") isn't a single shot of the sky, but a graphical and notional blend of the positions of the planets in the heavens, their location via signs, and their reference to one's location on Earth. The time of the horoscope event is taken in part from the rising sign degree, as seen in the position of the faster moving planets, such as the Sun throughout the day.

In the North Indian chart, the horoscope is read counterclockwise. The house positions stay in the same place in this chart, and the signs, which are numbered 1 to 12, rotate through the chart. Some people like this style because they prefer to be able to identify the houses quickly, and they believe that the shape of the horoscope is a yantra that brings additional blessings and power by gazing upon it.

The South Indian chart keeps the signs in the same place and moves the rising sign through the chart. The chart is read clockwise, which is how the planets look from the geocentric point of view. The South India chart is good for publishing purposes, as you are seeing with my preferences, in that the signs stay in the same boxes, making it easy to reference consistently.

From the sky to the horoscope: Transition of planets along the Earth-centered ecliptic into a horoscope diagram, which appears to look down at the planets from outer space.

To the right: The Elephant at the top shows the North Indian chart format where the houses stay constant and the signs move. It is read counterclockwise. The Elephant on the bottom shows the South Indian style where the signs remain in the same place and the houses change. It is read clockwise.

Guru, the planet Jupiter.

CHAPTER FIVE

RASIS: THE VEDIC SIGNS
OF THE ZODIAC

The wheel of time formed with 12 spokes
revolving round the heavens without wearing out.
— Aitareya Brahmana

I stated earlier that signs of the zodiac were a method for astrologers to make a grid in the sky where they could document planetary positions and use the information consistently in birth charts. The zodiac was a geometric division of the sky visually identified by astronomical marker stars. The 360-degree circle of the Sun, the ecliptic, was divided into 12 sections of 30 degrees each and originally given names similar to the star groups located nearby. A sign is called a *rasis,* which means a "heap" or a "quantity," in Vedic astrology—as in a heap or quantity of stars.

In order to understand the upcoming list of general descriptions of signs, it's important to know that each sign of the zodiac is associated with particular elements and qualities. The ancients symbolized the basic constituencies of our behavior and psychology in terms of five major elements. The very subtle element of *akasha,* or "space," is generally not considered in chart analysis—although it has qualities similar to the lightness of air. So the diversity of interactions in the cosmos can be grouped into four basic behaviors for creatures on Earth, related to the four main elements or "bhutas" of creation:

1. **Vayu (Air):** Mental approach; intellectual; artistic (Gemini, Libra, Aquarius)

2. **Tejas or Agni (Fire):** Fiery; energetic, innovative (Aries, Leo, Sagittarius)

3. **Prithivi or Bhoomi (Earth):** Stable; practical; conservative (Taurus, Virgo, Capricorn)

4. **Apas or Jal (Water):** Fluid emotions; intuitive; sympathetic (Cancer, Scorpio, Pisces)

In addition to the elements (bhutas), Vedic philosophy and astrology divide personalities and events into three types. These three operators are related to the three gunas described earlier. These qualities, taken together with the elements, form the building blocks of creation and give the astrologer further clues as to how a person's behavior can be identified through the horoscope. The three modes of operation in the process of creation and their related zodiac signs are:

1. **Chara** (chah' rah) **or Movable:** Changeable, active, innovative, travel (Aries, Cancer, Libra, Capricorn)

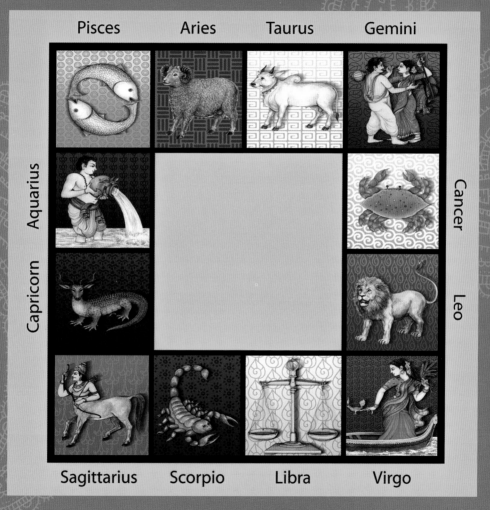

	Pisces	Aries	Taurus	Gemini	
Aquarius					Cancer
Capricorn					Leo
	Sagittarius	Scorpio	Libra	Virgo	

Each of the signs of the zodiac, called the rasis, are represented symbolically by created beings (such as animals, insects, and humans) and physical objects.

2. **Sthira** (sthih' rah) **or Fixed:** Stable, conservative, nonchanging (Taurus, Leo, Scorpio, Aquarius)

3. **Dwiswabhava** (dwish' wah bha' vha) **or Dual:** Qualities of both changeable and stable, flexible, adaptive, fickle (Gemini, Virgo, Sagittarius, Pisces)

With respect to gender: The odd signs are male, starting with Aries, and the even signs are female, beginning with Taurus. Male signs represent a more masculine, bold, and assertive quality; while female signs are more feminine, gentle, and supportive in nature.

It should be noted that the following information given for a sign can apply to the Lagna, the Moon, and the Sun. In fact, according to some established writers in Vedic astrology, deeper meaning can be derived from looking at the chart from the Lagna, then the Moon, then the Sun. The strength and favorableness of planets are synthesized from these three points and merged into a consolidated judgment of the chart—somewhat like taking three metals and combining them into a new alloy.

ARIES
Mesha (mesh' ah)

A Ram

Common Abbreviation: Ari

Symbol: A ram

Ruling Planet: Mars

Qualities: Moveable, fire, pitta

Key Concept: Getting things done; focus is on advancing oneself and taking action

Favorable Traits: Self-assertive; full of initiative; pioneering; courageous; active; loves adventure; childlike joy; gets things done

Unfavorable Traits: Adversarial; aggressive; impatient; uncooperative; jealous; reckless; leaves tasks undone

TAURUS
Vrishabha (vree shah' bah)

A Bull

Common Abbreviation: Tau

Symbol: A bull

Ruling Planet: Venus

Qualities: Fixed, earth, kapha

Key Concept: Keeping things stable; focus is on possessing

Favorable Traits: Productive; endurance; thorough; materialistic; tenacious; patient; steady; conservative; strong willed; loyal and true

Unfavorable Traits: Inflexible; boring; greedy; selfish; self-indulgent; slow to start; reactionary; intolerant; stubborn; jealous; overaccumulates

Gemini

Mithuna (mee too' nah)

A Female-Male Pair

Common Abbreviation: Gem

Symbol: A couple (maituna)—the male holding a club and the female holding a violinlike instrument called a *veena*. It's the convention in Western astrology, and among many modern Vedic astrologers, to use the symbol of twins.

Ruling Planet: Mercury

Qualities: Dual, air, vata

Key Concept: Making distinctions and communicating; focus is on thinking

Favorable Traits: Quick mind; handy; versatile; inventive; loves variety; genial; quick at making friends; trendy; debater; conversationalist or speaker; reading, writing, and oral skills

Unfavorable Traits: Indecisive; hasty; changeable; too clever; "two-faced"; conflicted; restless; nervous; flirtatious; inclined not to finish things; too much going on at once; fickle; irresponsible

CANCER
Karkata (kar kah' tah)

A Crab

Common Abbreviation: Can

Symbol: A crab

Ruling Planet: Moon

Qualities: Movable, water, kapha

Key Concept: Supporting the "family"; focus is on feelings

Favorable Traits: Love of home and family; instinctive; intuitive; imaginative; supportive; teacher; strong affections; loyal

Unfavorable Traits: Too dependent; doesn't know how to disengage; too available; lack of self-sufficiency; hoarder; hypersensitive; moody; feels abandoned; picks dysfunctional friends and partners

LEO
Simha (sim' hah)

A Lion

Common Abbreviation: Leo

Symbol: A lion

Ruling Planet: Sun

Qualities: Fixed, fire, pitta

Key Concept: Being the center of the universe; focus is on commanding and directing

Favorable Traits: Vital; leader; generous; dignified; skilled organizer; ambitious; fame and honor; willpower; large-issue oriented; delegates; flair for showmanship; self-promotion

Unfavorable Traits: Vain; arrogant; overbearing; opinionated; boasting; condescending; domineering; not detail oriented; spends beyond their means; power hunter; pompous

Virgo
Kanya (kahn' yah)

A Young Girl or Virgin

Common Abbreviation: Vir

Symbol: A young girl in a boat with a bundle of grains in one hand and a torch in the other

Ruling Planet: Mercury

Qualities: Dual, earth, vata

Key Concept: Perfection through purifying; focus is on serving, protecting, and improving

Favorable Traits: Analytical; oriented to serving; studious; high standards; purifies and improves things to their ideal state; sensitive; reserved; commercial instinct; detailed and methodical; skilled in letters, numbers, and measuring

Unfavorable Traits: Sets expectations too high; too narrow a focus; worried; frustrated; skeptical; fault-finding; too literal; boring; lonely; lack of self-promotion

LIBRA
Tula (too' lah)

A Scale

Common Abbreviation: Lib

Symbol: Balance scales

Ruling Planet: Venus

Qualities: Moveable, air, kapha

Key Concept: Balancing and resolving opposites; focus is on harmony

Favorable Traits: Reassuring; inspiring; adaptable; positive; diplomatic; can see both sides; flair for fashion; balanced; graceful; skill as a middleman

Unfavorable Traits: Ambivalent; too adjusting or compromising; avoids conflict or responsibility; manipulative; capricious; ineffectual; vacillates; says yes to everybody; chameleon

Scorpio
Vrishchika (vrish' chick ah)

A Scorpion

Common Abbreviation: Sco

Symbol: A scorpion

Ruling Planet: Mars

Qualities: Fixed, water, pitta

Key Concept: Obtaining through transforming, seducing or investigating; focus is on the unknown

Favorable Traits: Devoted; pleasure giving; deep level of feeling; highly intuitive; deep spiritual base; healing capacity; works well by instinct

Unfavorable Traits: Critical, possessive, vengeful, hypersensitive; speaks ill of others; controlling; punishing; worrier; grim outlook; takes "patients" as partners; victimized in love; gets intimate too quickly

Sagittarius
Dhanus (dahn' oos)

A Bow

Common Abbreviation: Sag

Symbol: An archer who is half man and half horse

Ruling Planet: Jupiter

Qualities: Dual, fire, pitta

Key Concept: Striving for freedom and fairness; focus is on justice

Favorable Traits: Idealistic; courageous; self-confident; vigorous; loves truth; needs to be told the reason behind things; ethical, humanitarian concerns; benefits from constant mental and physical stimulation

Unfavorable Traits: Zealot; fanatic; pushy; greedy; lacks tact; needs frequent changes; unreliable; quick tempered

Capricorn
Makara (mah' kah rah)

A Crocodile-like Sea Monster

Common Abbreviation: Cap

Symbol: A creature with the head of a deer and the body of a crocodile

Ruling Planet: Saturn

Qualities: Movable, earth, vata

Key Concept: Prospering through enduring; focus is on security

Favorable Traits: Practical; methodical; persevering; organizing ability; serves others well; prefers seclusion and peace; loyal

Unfavorable Traits: Suspicious; cruel; selfish; pessimistic; slow to act; depressed by obstacles and delays; overworks and strains; gloomy; too detached; lack of affection

Aquarius
Kumbha (koom' bha)

A Water Pot

Common Abbreviation: Aqu

Symbol: A man pouring from a water pot

Ruling Planet: Saturn

Qualities: Fixed, earth, vata

Key Concept: Believing in the Ideal; focus is on innovation

Favorable Traits: Scientific; humane; innovative; intuitive; political interests; shrewd; sympathetic; accommodating

Unfavorable Traits: Impractical; doesn't recognize own talents; too shy; unconventional; outspoken; needs more routine; doesn't fit in; too secretive; paranoid

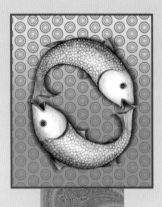

PISCES
Meena (meen' ah)

Fish

Common Abbreviation: Pis

Symbol: Two fish, side by side, swimming in opposite directions

Ruling Planet: Jupiter

Qualities: Dual, water, kapha

Key Concept: The stream of consciousness flowing back and forth between heaven and earth; focus is on believing and the spiritual world

Favorable Traits: Mystical; intuitive; philosophical; contemplative; comforting; attracted to the concepts of enlightenment and liberation

Unfavorable Traits: Procrastinates; disconnected thinking; lacks confidence; naive; poor financial planner; appears weak or defenseless; not interested enough

Rising Signs

The signs of the zodiac relate to the planet Earth starting from a place called the *rising sign*. This actual point on the horizon marking the first sign (and house) in an individual chart is called the ascendant, or *Lagna* (which translates to "attached to") of the horoscope. The signs in the heavens connect to the earth at this point—the celestial and the terrestrial join forces. The Lagna is also the first house and is very important in determining the *bala,* or overall "strength," as well as the temperament of the person or event represented by the chart.

It's important to understand that the Lagna, or rising sign, gives a summary, a bio of sorts, about the general traits and disposition of an individual or event. I think that at least 60 to 70 percent of the nature or personality of a person can be seen through the traits carried by the rising sign, its occupants, its ruler, and whether that ruler is favorably placed and aspected or not.

The rising sign and its degree determines the rest of the chart, including the house placements of all the planets. It's important to note in Vedic astrology that the "cusp" of the rising sign or first house of the chart is the middle point of the house (*bhava madhya*—pronounced "bhah' vah mah' dyah")—not the end. The middle of a house is strong and the beginning and end points (*sandhi,* "sahn' dee") are weak. After the rising sign is calculated, usually through a software program, the remainder of the signs are placed in sequence around the circle of the zodiac. Again, this is done in a clockwise manner in the South India chart and in a counterclockwise direction in the North India chart style. In most Western wheel charts, the circle of the signs is read in a counterclockwise manner.

Another important consideration about the 12 rising signs is that they each will generate a favorable or unfavorable relationship to the planets participating in the rest of that chart. This is often due to specific planets being friends (helpful) or enemies (obstructing) of the rising sign ruler. We also see that those planets' influences are modified in favorableness (or not) according to which house they rule or occupy. The rising sign ruler is almost always favorable since the Lagna is a trine and angle both. The *trikona* (tree' koh nah) or trines signs/houses (1, 5, and 9) and kendra (kehn' drah) or angle signs/houses (1, 4, 7, and 10) are favorable, in general, and the dusthanas (doosh' tah nah) (houses 6, 8, and 12) are generally unfavorable.

Goddess holding moon and creating an eclipse.

Shukra, the planet Venus.

CHAPTER SIX

VEDIC HOUSES AND PLANETARY RULERSHIPS

*A single astrologer who studies the course of Destiny, who is familiar
with the special features of times and climes, can achieve what a thousand
elephants and four times as many horses cannot together do.*
— Varahamihira

I explained earlier, in the section on chart formats, how the 12 houses are used in concert with the 12 signs (and in Vedic astrology, with the divisional charts and the nakshatras). Houses are the containers of signs and planets. They're like a 12-room cosmic hotel where the signs and planets can come down to Earth and do something. They deliver the karma they contain for each person according to the nature of the house and sign they're both visiting, ruling, ruled by, and according to the nature of the planets they're sharing space with. This is similar to how we're all conditioned by where we live, who is in charge of that space, and how well we interact with our neighbors and they with us.

The Sanskrit word *bhava,* or what we call a house, translates to "state of existence," or in some cases, "a mood." The planets have a place to exist (a house to live in) and, again, while each planet has its own identity, its basic nature is modified by taking on the mood or characteristics of the house it occupies. For example, if Venus, which identifies how and what we love, is located in the fourth house, we might love family matters more. If Venus is in the second house, we might like accumulating money more.

Each house is occupied by or linked to a sign in each chart, and that sign is ruled by a specific planet. Thus, a house is associated with both a sign and a ruling planet and takes on those two influences for the good or bad. Houses, signs, and planets all interact in the birth chart forming the unique identity of a person or event. Planetary rulers of the sign, planets in the house, and the conjunctions and aspects they form with other planets in the chart strongly influence the houses, their traits or indications, and the area of life they rule. The houses particularize the chart because they deal with a specific time and place and give the signs somewhere to go.

Another Vedic technique you might want to explore is called *Bhavat Bhavan* (bah' vaht bhah' vahn) by most Vedic astrologers, and tells us that the indications for a specific house can be judged from the same distance from that house as that house is from the Lagna (that's a mouthful!). For example, if we want to find out about our mother-in-law—that is, our wife's mother—we would look four houses (the fourth represents the mother) from the house of the spouse, which is the seventh. This would give us the tenth house, counting the seventh house as one, and going four places from there to the tenth. That's where we can see indications in the chart about the nature of our mother-in-law. We could also broaden our research by looking at our wife's or partner's fourth house to gain more insight about the mother-in-law. We can do this with any indication (karaka) as long as we know what house and number it stands for and count from there.

The rules for interpreting houses are given in Chapter 8, which covers chart calculation. For now, *kendras,* or "angles" (1, 4, 7, and 10) and trikonas (1, 5, and 9) are favorable. The Lagna, or first house, especially its ruler, is generally very favorable since it's both an angle and a trine.

Houses 6, 8, and 12 (dusthanas) are deemed unfavorable. The planets occupying or ruling these houses are said to have their unfavorable effects magnified. Some say, however, that a dusthana ruler in a dusthana house could actually be favorable, theorizing that an unfavorable planet is weakened there.

House 3 is somewhat unfavorable since it's eighth to the eighth (per Bhavat Bhavam). Houses 2 and 11 are financial houses and good for that reason. The ruler of the 11th is not counted as

Determining houses: For any time and place on Earth, the sign of the zodiac rising on the eastern horizon is called the first house. All the other houses are evenly spaced out from there in 30-degree equal segments, around the birth chart diagram. The Sun will be in the first house (or rising sign) each morning at dawn, and will move through all the houses like "clockwork," in about a day. The Sun will move through all the signs in about a year.

favorable (for one thing, it's 6th from the 6th house, the house of illness and ene-mies—again per Bhavat Bhavam).

There are exceptions to the rule, called *upachaya* (oo' pah chay' ah) or "growing houses"—3, 6, 10, and 11, and their rulers and occupants, are considered to get better over time.

There are other house categories, such as *panapharas* (pah' nah pah' rahs) (2, 5, 8, and 11, or cadents), apoklimas (ah' pohk lee' mahs) (3, 6, 9, and 12, or succeedents), but we don't need to use them at this starter level.

First House
Tanu (tah' noo) Bhava, the House of the Body

Keywords: The physical self; personality; vitality

Basic Nature: Favorable; generally the most important house in the chart

Relates to: The sign of Aries and the planet Mars

Signifies: Appearance; basic disposition; vitality; general physical and emotional well-being

Favorable Traits: Good health, strength, appearance, and overall demeanor. The *bala,* or "strength," is high when the ruler of the 1st is favorably placed in the 1st, or in angles (4, 7, or 10) or trines (5 and 9), is conjunct or aspected by other benefic planets and is in other favorable houses, such as the 2nd and 11th (money houses), or the 3rd, which is generally about courage and determination—although some

First House, Tanu (tah' noo) Bhava, the House of the Body.

Second House, Dhana (dah' nah) Bhava, the House of Accumulated Wealth.

astrologers are concerned it could be too aggressive or unpleasant, thus malefic. It also strengths the first house (which is also the rising sign) if it's occupied or aspected by benefic planets.

Unfavorable Traits: Strength, health, confidence, and capacity to thrive are challenged if there are negative influences coming to this house. The bala is thus low, and the person is more vulnerable to negative circumstances, especially if the ruler of the 1st house is also unfavorably placed, such as in the dusthanas (6, 8, and 12th houses) or conjunct a malefic planet, or if a dusthana ruler is located in or aspects the 1st or is placed in a weak position in a sign (such as debilitated, sandhi, and so forth).

Second House
Dhana (dah' nah) Bhava, the House of Accumulated Wealth

Keywords: Accumulation of possessions and finances; liquid assets; food; speech

Basic Nature: A mix of favorable and unfavorable, since its ruler isn't regarded as favorable (a *maraka* or "killer" planet); this is where you see how well you accumulate money

Relates to: The sign of Taurus and the planet Venus

Signifies: General family happiness; food and drink; speaking and languages; liquid assets (currency, precious metals, gems, and the like); accumulation of wealth; ability to study and pay attention; truthfulness and right speech; body region of right eye, face (from eyebrows down to collarbone), mouth (lips, tongue, teeth, and gums), front of neck; thyroid area

Favorable Traits: Good finances and prosperous accumulation of liquid assets (such as currency, cash, gems, precious metals, stock certificates); general family happiness; bountiful food and nourishment; good voice and effective speech; studies well, persists, and pays attention

Unfavorable Traits: Trouble through speech; family discord; problems accumulating sufficient financial resources; difficulties around food; attention deficit; poor study habits

THIRD HOUSE
Sahaja (sah hah' jah) Bhava, the House of Siblings

Keywords: Determination; courage; siblings; neighbors

Basic Nature: A mix between favorable and unfavorable; many authors regard it as unfavorable since it represents effort and is the 8th house located away from the 8th house—the house of death. Note that in Vedic astrology, you can treat any planet or house and what it signifies as if it were the 1st house and make an analysis from there. As I indicated earlier, some astrologers call this technique *Bhavat Bhavan.* Both these word are terms for the same word, "existence" or "being."

Relates to: The sign of Gemini and the planet Mercury

Third House, Sahaja (sah hah' jah) Bhava, the House of Siblings.

Fourth House, Matru (mah' troo) Bhava, the House of the Mother.

Signifies: Siblings; neighbors; courage; physical strength; sales and marketing; self-expression through art, dance, drama, music, singing, and related arts; speaker; writer; communicator; benefits from adventure and fun; body areas related to hearing, ear diseases, arms, hands, back of neck and shoulders, nervous system and respiration

Favorable Traits: Courageous; self-directed; persuasive and communicative; applies themselves; treats others as their "brother or sister"; good at self-expression through the arts, such as dance, music, drama, writing, and communication

Unfavorable Traits: Lack of courage or direction; too aggressive; trouble with siblings and neighbors; poor in self-expression and communication; puts in too much effort or not enough

FOURTH HOUSE
Matru (mah' troo) Bhava, the House of the Mother

Keywords: Mothering; feelings; home; fixed assets; education

Basic Nature: Favorable

Relates to: The sign of Cancer and the Moon

Signifies: Mother; knowledge; education; fixed assets; the home; shelter; clothing; real estate; vehicles; emotions; happiness in general; instructing and informing others; sense of community and the public; things from below the earth; region of the chest, breasts, and heart area

Favorable Traits: Motherly; good teacher or counselor; intuitive; social skills; benefits from good home and happy family; emotionally rich; gets comforts; good fixed assets (home, vehicles, high-cost acquisitions, etc.)

Unfavorable Traits: Emotional; hypersensitive; too changeable; ungrounded; trouble getting fixed assets (home, car, and the like); insufficient or incomplete education; not nurturing; hoards or is selfish; socially insensitive or unskilled

FIFTH HOUSE
Putra (poo' trah) Bhava, the House of Children

Keywords: Children; intelligence; romance; youthful behavior; speculation

Basic Nature: Favorable

Relates to: The sign of Leo and the Sun

Signifies: Children; pregnancy; romance; love from spouse or sweetheart; speculation, spiritual techniques (especially meditation); knowledge of shastras or scriptures; past-life credit *(purva punya)*; intelligence; discrimination; games, amusements, and sports; business; royal favor; region of the heart and circulatory system

Favorable Traits: Good intellect; discriminating; playful or sporty; entertaining, entertainer, or celebrity in their field; interest in higher knowledge; business skills; knows how to take a measured risk; romantic and thoughtful; benefits from children

Fifth House, Putra (poo' trah) Bhava, the House of Children.

Sixth House, Ripu (ree' poo) or Roga (roh' gah) Bhava, the House of Enemies or Disease.

Unfavorable Traits: Lack of discrimination; dishonest; lack of romance; difficulty meditating; doesn't test well; poor business sense; trouble through children; speculation problems; lack of fun or entertainment

Sixth House
Ripu (ree' poo) or Roga (roh' gah) Bhava, the House of Enemies or Disease

Keywords: Service; defense; servants/co-workers; opponents; accidents; short illness

Basic Nature: Unfavorable, although it can get better over time (*upachaya,* or "growing")

Relates to: The sign of Virgo and the planet Mercury

Signifies: Uncles and aunts (mother's siblings); warriors; healers; emergency care; protecting and serving; competitors; opposition; litigation; enemies; struggles; pets; servants or helpers; employees; thefts; region of abdomen and bowels; wounds, injuries, and accidents

Favorable Traits: Warrior by nature; protector; guardian; healer; protects the interests of others (police, legal, armed services); office work and service business; benefits through enemies

Unfavorable Traits: Combative; angry disposition; impatient; at odds with others; poor service provider or bad employee; troubled by enemies, accidents, and injuries

Seventh House
Kalatra (kah lah' trah) Bhava, the House of the Partner

Keywords: Partnerships; relationships with others; dealings

Basic Nature: Favorable, though its ruler isn't regarded as favorable by some, being a *maraka,* or "killer" planet

Relates to: The sign of Libra and the planet Venus

Signifies: Partnerships, marriage, or marriage-like relationships; contracts with others; love affairs; trade; middle men; diplomacy; regions of the body associated with waist and lower back, kidneys, and liver area

Favorable Traits: Diplomatic; builds rapport; adaptable; understands others well; mimic; helps others achieve balance; business sense; intermediary of all sorts; legal contracts

Unfavorable Traits: Shifty; unpredictable moods; unreliable; out of balance; overly accommodating; difficulty being straightforward; avoids confrontation too much; trouble with commitments; poor at business

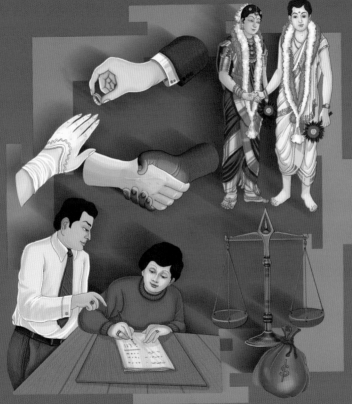

Seventh House, Kalatra (kah lah' trah) Bhava, the House of the Partner.

Eighth House, Ayu (ah' yoo) Bhava, the House of Life.

Eighth House

Ayu (ah' yoo) Bhava, the House of Life

Keywords: The unknown or transcendental; investigating, transforming; support/resources; chronic illness

Basic Nature: Unfavorable; perhaps the worst of the unfavorables; but still possibly okay

Relates to: The sign of Scorpio and the planet Mars

Signifies: Knowledge of the unknown or mystical matters; investigations; intuition and instincts; scandal, embarrassment, and shame; shyness; lack of self-promotion; unearned wealth (lotteries, legacies, etc.); worry; vitality and sexual energy; cheating; accusations; death, dying, and matters about end of life; longevity; chronic ailments; reproductive and elimination systems

Favorable Traits: Investigative; good at getting the support of others and giving it, too; skilled in mystical, transcendental, and hidden pursuits; healer; advance intuition; adept at issues dealing with life extension, health, vitality, and old age; finds the beauty in ugliness

Unfavorable Traits: Lives off others' good graces; fearful; focused on negative outcomes; oversexed; not healthy; hypochondriac; phobic; doesn't take care of themselves; negative mental states

Ninth House

Bhagya (bah' gyah) Bhava, the House of Fortune;
also Dharma (dar' mah) Bhava, the House of Right Action

Keywords: Fortune; higher knowledge; philosophy; guru; long travels

Basic Nature: Very favorable; one of the best

Relates to: The sign of Sagittarius and the planet Jupiter

Signifies: Father; God; guru; philosophy; religion; good fortune; right action or dharma; ethics; law; long-distance travel; divine grace (5th from 5th); institutions of higher learning; initiation; connection with Divine powers or energies (devas); region of the body associated with thighs and upper leg

Favorable Traits: Ability to give and receive higher knowledge; ethical; just; fortunate; gets good guru and other types of advisers; benefits from long-distance travel

Unfavorable Traits: Spiritual poser or teacher of incorrect knowledge; unfortunate; trouble with father and guru; long-distance travel is problematic

Tenth House

Karma (kar' mah) Bhava, the House of Action

Keyword: Career; status; life purpose

Basic Nature: Favorable

Ninth House, Bhagya (bah' gyah) Bhava, the House of Fortune;
also Dharma (dar' mah) Bhava, the House of Right Action.

Tenth House, Karma (kar' mah) Bhava, the House of Action.

Relates to: The sign of Capricorn and the planet Saturn

Signifies: Life purpose or career; fame; status or reputation; father's reputation or position in the world; character; business; represents the region around the knees

Favorable Traits: Good business success; focused; dedicated; finds a way to make things work; good reputation and character

Unfavorable Traits: Trouble with business; questionable business practices and reputation; lack of attention to business activities; doesn't prosper well in career or show sufficient interest for success

Eleventh House
Labya (lah' byah) Bhava, the House of Gains

Keywords: Opportunities; profits; cash flow; friends and allies

Basic Nature: All planets are considered good here, but the ruler of this house isn't well regarded by many astrologers, so this house is considered a mix of favorable and unfavorable

Relates to: The sign of Aquarius and the planet Saturn

Signifies: Cash flow; hopes; dreams; friends; influential friends; elder sibling; left ear

Favorable Traits: Money flows in well; has good friends and is a good friend; benefits from influential people; elder sibling is a help; is able to realize dreams

Unfavorable Traits: Trouble with cash flow; unreliable or unfortunate friends; eldest sibling faces difficulties; not a good friend; has trouble getting what they want; dreams don't get realized, or come late or in small quantity

Twelfth House
Moksha (mohk' shah) Bhava, the House of Enlightenment

Keywords: Liberation; loss; faraway and mystical places

Basic Nature: Not favorable for material life, but good for the spiritual

Relates to: The sign of Pisces and the planet Jupiter

Signifies: Many spiritual seekers have strong connections to this house, such as ruler of the 1st in the 12th, ruler of the 10th in the 12th, Sun or Moon in the 12th, strong planets in the 12th; liberation; moksha or enlightenment; sexual pleasures; places of confinement (hospitals, clinics, prisons, ashrams, long-term meditation retreats, etc.); loss; poverty; disinterest in the material world; generosity; quality of sleep and beds; self-sacrifice; spiritual journeys; pilgrimages or journeys to foreign lands; wandering; trade involving long travel; life after death; the nature of one's previous incarnation; martyrs; victims; clumsiness

Favorable Traits: Spiritual seeker; refined nature; works for the world in some humanitarian, spiritual, or educational manner; charity worker; fund-raiser; leads others to liberation

Eleventh House, Labya (lah' byah) Bhava, the House of Gains.

Twelfth House, Moksha (mohk' shah) Bhava, the House of Enlightenment.

Unfavorable Traits: Too disinterested to gain enough finances; overly generous; loses through giving too much of themselves or their resources; victim; martyr; feels betrayed; people take advantage of their kindness; lack of direction and self-promotion

Now that I've explained the 12 houses of Vedic astrology, we're ready to explore those planets that rule the signs that the houses are located in. These are in effect called the rulers or lords of each house, since in many cases the sign and house are treated as one in Vedic astrology.

Adhipatis: Planetary Rulerships

All signs have one assigned ruler. But since there are nine planets and a dozen signs, with the exception of Moon (Cancer ruled) and Sun (Leo ruled), the planets rule two signs each. The traits of the planetary ruler of a sign are said to be comparable to the characteristics of that sign. The planet owning a sign disposes that sign to act in the nature of that planet. The sign will also act according to how that dispositor, as it's called, is located elsewhere in the chart, and what planets are conjunct or aspecting it. If a ruler of a house (remember—signs and houses occupy the same place in a Vedic chart) is favorably placed, then that house and its characteristics will come forward in a more positive fashion. If the ruler isn't well placed, then the house it rules will be troubled by the affliction to its ruler.

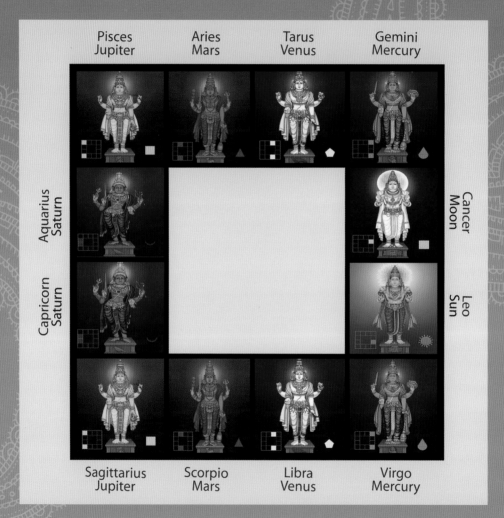

Pisces
Jupiter

Aries
Mars

Tarus
Venus

Gemini
Mercury

Aquarius
Saturn

Cancer
Moon

Capricorn
Saturn

Leo
Sun

Sagittarius
Jupiter

Scorpio
Mars

Libra
Venus

Virgo
Mercury

Planets rule signs, and each sign reflects the nature and traits of the planet ruling it.

Planets in Signs and Houses

We've discussed planets, planets ruling houses, planets being ruled or "disposited" by other planets, and planets in combination or aspect with other planets. When you know the planets and what they indicate—that is, their *karakas*—along with their strength and favorableness, you have the key to the chart.

The descriptions of the planets located in the various signs and houses will also give you further detail about the nature and quality of the chart and its significations. As mentioned earlier, a planet in a sign will be influenced by the planet ruling that sign. Again, if Saturn is in Virgo, we can say that Saturn is in Mercury's sign. We can also say that this Saturn/Mercury combination is further modified by Virgo's traits as the sixth sign of the zodiac. We can look at this combination in terms of sixth-house characteristics. To help you with this, in the following material, I've put each combination next to the title of each planet in a sign, along with the house the sign symbolizes. You can combine the keyword associated with each of these to make simple interpretive statements.

Surya (Sun) planetary yantra.

THE SUN IN SIGNS

Sun in Aries (Sun/Mars/1st)
Favorable: Ambitious; courageous; warrior; competitive; executive
Unfavorable: Aggressive; harsh; impatient

Sun in Taurus (Sun/Venus/2nd)
Favorable: Focus; stamina; accumulates well; money grows over time
Unfavorable: Stubborn; stuck; possessive

Sun in Gemini (Sun/Mercury/3rd)
Favorable: Verbal and writing skills; friendly; communicative; innovative; inquisitive
Unfavorable: Divided; not dependable; vacillates; nervous; naive

Sun in Cancer (Sun/Moon/4th)
Favorable: Imaginative; instinctual; works well in groups; caring
Unfavorable: Fickle; scattered; too emotional; sentimental

Sun in Leo (Sun/Sun/5th)
Favorable: Fatherly; in charge; charismatic; influential; leader
Unfavorable: Vain; weakness for flattery; insecure; pretentious; controlling; too superior

Sun in Virgo (Sun/Mercury/6th)
Favorable: Analytical; orderly; protective; precise; numerical and administrative disposition
Unfavorable: Critical; sets criteria too high; overworks; disappointed in themselves and others

Sun in Libra (Sun/Venus/7th)
Favorable: Accommodating; achieves balance; gracious; artful and creative; counselor
Unfavorable: Out of balance; indecisive; not dependable; deceptive; unproductive

Sun in Scorpio (Sun/Mars/8th)
Favorable: Purposeful; helps others improve; mystical; transcendental knowledge
Unfavorable: Forceful; domineering; controlling; jealous; secretive; cruel

Sun in Sagittarius (Sun/Jupiter/9th)
Favorable: Champion of justice and fair play; educator; counselor; lover of freedom; ethical
Unfavorable: Defiant; reckless; changes too much; lack of steady growth

Sun in Capricorn (Sun/Saturn/10th)
Favorable: Dependable; loyal; hard worker; gains through conservation; structured; steady
Unfavorable: Works too hard; heartless; regretful; taken advantage of by others

Sun in Aquarius (Sun/Saturn/11th)
Favorable: Pursues justice; inventive; political skills; philosophic; friendly
Unfavorable: Odd; doesn't fit in; too idealistic; upset by political action

Sun in Pisces (Sun/Jupiter/12th)
Favorable: Philanthropist; counselor; spiritual interests; interest in the past and causes for things
Unfavorable: Ineffective; hopeless; too dreamy

Chandra (Moon) planetary yantra.

The Moon in Signs

Moon in Aries (Moon/Mars/1st)
Favorable: Motivated; responds quickly; charming; warrior energy
Unfavorable: Quick change in feelings; too seductive; undependable; cruel; impatient

Moon in Taurus (Moon/Venus/2nd)
Favorable: Popular; steady emotions; dependable; comforting; makes others secure
Unfavorable: Stubborn; rigid; reactionary; hoards; sticks with the wrong people

Moon in Gemini (Moon/Mercury/3rd)
Favorable: Friendly; charming speaker; witty; innovative; youthful
Unfavorable: Vacillates; undependable; divided; copies others; can't decide

Moon in Cancer (Moon/Moon/4th)
Favorable: Concerns for friends and family; intuitive; nurturing; imaginative; social skills
Unfavorable: Doesn't know how to disengage; victim of love; fickle; hypersensitive

Moon in Leo (Moon/Sun/5th)
Favorable: Concerned for the welfare of others; gracious; ceremonious; proud; leader
Unfavorable: Quick to take offense; builds their identity on others' opinions; vain; arrogant

Moon in Virgo (Moon/Mercury/6th)
Favorable: Modest; proper; reserved; honest; protective; defends principles and ideals
Unfavorable: Critical; picky; erratic; too mental; lack of emotional connection; calculating

Moon in Libra (Moon/Venus/7th)
Favorable: Intermediary; peacemaker; balancer; fair; lover of beauty and pleasure
Unfavorable: Too laissez-faire; keeps changing approach; taken advantage of; afraid to confront

Moon in Scorpio (Moon/Mars/8th)

Favorable: Straight talker; cares deeply; investigative; transforming; intuitive; mystic; sensual

Unfavorable: Offended easily; vindictive; blunt; harsh; impatient; cruel; secretive; indulgent

Moon in Sagittarius (Moon/Jupiter/9th)

Favorable: Open-minded; influential; popular; freedom fighter; ideal driven; enthusiastic

Unfavorable: Irritating speech; severe ideals; doesn't know when to back off; too direct

Moon in Capricorn (Moon/Saturn/10th)

Favorable: Clever; finds a way; organized; methodical; responsible; steadfast; faithful

Unfavorable: Too crafty; hard to know or trust; regretful; depressed; pessimistic; heartless

Moon in Aquarius (Moon/Saturn/11th)

Favorable: Political skill, courteous; friendly; keeps confidences; philosophic

Unfavorable: Weird concepts; out of touch; too political; intense; depressed; low self-esteem

Moon in Pisces (Moon/Jupiter/12th)

Favorable: Soft-spoken, spiritual; charitable; fond of pleasure; intuitive; philosophical

Unfavorable: Too easily moved; too sensitive; vacillates; ineffective; unproductive

Mangala (Mars) planetary yantra.

Mars in Signs

Mars in Aries (Mars/Mars/1st)
Favorable: Executive; warrior; quick decisions; courageous; protective; energetic
Unfavorable: Fickle; intimate too quickly; rash; easily irritated; fighting mind

Mars in Taurus (Mars/Venus/2nd)

Favorable: Charming; quick action; dependable leader; protects others
Unfavorable: Digs in too quickly; possessive; too desirous; harsh speech; reckless

Mars in Gemini (Mars/Gemini/3rd)

Favorable: Quick thinker, speaker and writer; fast reflexes; imaginative; rapid responder
Unfavorable: Jumps to conclusions; vacillates; undependable; hesitant, then decides too fast

Mars in Cancer (Mars/Moon/4th)

Favorable: Quick to respond; adaptable emotions; socially adept; care quickly
Unfavorable: Emotionally undependable; annoyed by weakness; flairs up; feels restrained in love

Mars in Leo (Mars/Sun/5th)

Favorable: Takes the lead quickly; decisive; fast reaction time; competitive; sporty
Unfavorable: Aggressive; impatient; arrogant; acts too quickly; trouble with authorities

Mars in Virgo (Mars/Virgo/6th)

Favorable: Fast thinker; analytical; decisive; eager; breakthrough thinker
Unfavorable: Critical; impatient; mind full of chatter; decides without enough information

Mars in Libra (Mars/Venus/7th)

Favorable: Charming; charismatic; appealing; quick artistry; deals quickly
Unfavorable: Undependable; too sensual; dissolute, immodest; uncommitted; too clever

Mars in Scorpio (Mars/Mars/8th)

Favorable: Rugged; energetic; reacts quickly; warrior; protective; youthful; vigorous

Unfavorable: Easily irritated; inconsiderate; overreacts; looks without leaping; no exit strategy

Mars in Sagittarius (Mars/Jupiter/9th)

Favorable: Fond of justice; protector of the weak; makes money quickly; full of opportunity

Unfavorable: Creates conflicts and opposition; trouble with the law; financial losses; rebellious

Mars in Capricorn (Mars/Saturn/10th)

Favorable: Influential power; smart; effective; valuable worker

Unfavorable: Works in spurts; inconsistent; bored easily; doesn't complete things; too aggressive

Mars in Aquarius (Mars/Saturn/11th)

Favorable: Industrious; energetic; focuses to fulfill desires; balances energy and direction

Unfavorable: Hyper; tired to point of depression; traumatized; hurtful

Mars in Pisces (Mars/Jupiter/12th)

Favorable: Feels deeply and passionately; enthusiastic; inspiring; energizes others

Unfavorable: Restless; falls into temptation quickly; wasteful; ethical troubles; quick to judge

Budha (Mercury) planetary yantra.

Mercury in Signs

Mercury in Aries (Mercury/Mars/1st)
Favorable: Quick problem solver; mentally alert; efficient speech; motivator
Unfavorable: Unscrupulous; deceptive; mental agitation; fast-talker; accusative

Mercury in Taurus (Mercury/Venus/2nd)

Favorable: Creative; acquisitive; charismatic; imaginative; speaking and writing skills

Unfavorable: Fickle; untrustworthy; embellishes the truth; copycat; jealous of others' ideas

Mercury in Gemini (Mercury/Mercury/3rd)

Favorable: Studious; clever speech; tactful; innovative; quick intellect

Unfavorable: Deceitful; too mental; talks too much; doesn't take action; charms their way

Mercury in Cancer (Mercury/Moon/4th)

Favorable: Imaginative; writing and speaking skills; comforting talk; ingenious; teacher

Unfavorable: Fragmented; too much going on; mental confusion; imagines negative things

Mercury in Leo (Mercury/Mercury/5th)

Favorable: Clever; influential thinker and speaker; organizer; creative leader; thinks big

Unfavorable: Conceited; overevaluates their worth; vain; impractical thinking

Mercury in Virgo (Mercury/Mercury/6th)

Favorable: Learned; smart; respected thinker; conscientious; speaker and writer; organized

Unfavorable: Thinks the life out of things; analysis paralysis; complicated ideas; can't execute

Mercury in Libra (Mercury/Venus/7th)
Favorable: Creative; imaginative; considerate; genial; philosophical; weighs their words
Unfavorable: Builds castles in the air; impractical; waits too much to be inspired; indulgent

Mercury in Scorpio (Mercury/Mars/8th)
Favorable: Decisive; influential; sharp and quick thinking; takes action
Unfavorable: Enigmatic; too secretive; depressed; lacks certainty; reckless; speedy; critical

Mercury in Sagittarius (Mercury/Jupiter/9th)
Favorable: Oriented to justice, virtue, and fair play; creative thinker; thoughts of abundance
Unfavorable: Doesn't consider the details; emotions cloud the thinking; naive; overconfident

Mercury in Capricorn (Mercury/Saturn/10th)
Favorable: Organized mind; dedicated; loyal; sticks to the truth; honors traditions
Unfavorable: Pessimistic; liar; obsessive; dull; irreligious; uncaring; stuck; unenthusiastic

Mercury in Aquarius (Mercury/Saturn/11th)

Favorable: Creative focus; innovative compulsion; high level of concentration; structured

Unfavorable: Stuck; obsessive-compulsive; depressed; feels powerless

Mercury in Pisces (Mercury/Jupiter/12th)

Favorable: Innovative thinker; philosophical; intuitive; creative writing and speaking

Unfavorable: Thinks of failing; not focused enough; worrisome; distracted; easily annoyed

Guru (Jupiter) planetary yantra.

Jupiter in Signs

Jupiter in Aries (Jupiter/Mars/1st)
Favorable: Expansive actions; dynamic philosophy; prosperity
Unfavorable: Extravagant; supports unfounded philosophies; not ethical; trouble with law

Jupiter in Taurus (Jupiter/Venus/2nd)

Favorable: Creative; artistic; instructive speech; positive; builds up finances; collector

Unfavorable: Wasteful; lack of stamina; indulgent; poor money planning; uneconomical

Jupiter in Gemini (Jupiter/Mercury/3rd)

Favorable: Writing, speaking, lecturing; instructs and informs; publishing; working with children

Unfavorable: Inconsiderate speech and writing; thinks more than acts

Jupiter in Cancer (Jupiter/Moon/4th)

Favorable: Prosperity; good education; counselor; ethical; spiritual; positive expansion in family

Unfavorable: Overconfident; reacts too slowly to opportunities; indulgent; takes too much leisure

Jupiter in Leo (Jupiter/Sun/5th)

Favorable: High-level knowledge provider; good executive skill; positive; gives others hope

Unfavorable: Self-absorbed; taken in by false gurus or teachers; unproductive; ostentatious

Jupiter in Virgo (Jupiter/Mercury/6th)

Favorable: Good writing and speaking skills; precise philosophies; successful planner; spiritual

Unfavorable: Critical of spirituality; lacks attention to detail; too confident in their own mind

Jupiter in Libra (Jupiter/Venus/7th)

Favorable: Artistic; expansive; kind; supportive; counselor or teacher; inspirational; prosperous

Unfavorable: Indulgent; lethargic; lack of motivation; overconfident; lack of initiative

Jupiter in Scorpio (Jupiter/Mars/8th)

Favorable: Motivational; successful endeavors; effective; dynamic; prosperous outcomes

Unfavorable: Careless; expands too quickly; misses opportunities or doesn't focus on wealth

Jupiter in Sagittarius (Jupiter/Jupiter/9th)

Favorable: Blessed life; good spirituality; helps others; teacher/counselor; prosperity; positive

Unfavorable: Incompetent; unmotivated or lazy; uninspired; naive; immature

Jupiter in Capricorn (Jupiter/Saturn/10th)

Favorable: Focused expansion; simplicity; traditional views; conservative; spiritual; loyal

Unfavorable: Feels lack of prosperity; low finances; unscrupulous; unprincipled; slow growth

Jupiter in Aquarius (Jupiter/Saturn/11th)

Favorable: Focus on philosophy; innovative; structured expansion; political advocate

Unfavorable: Frustrated; follows wrong causes; too political; immobilized; setbacks to growth

Jupiter in Pisces (Jupiter/Jupiter/12th)

Favorable: Drawn to philosophy and religion; inspirational; ethical; just, generous

Unfavorable: Follows blindly; lack of spiritual competency; poser; idle; oversimplifies

Shukra (Venus) planetary yantra.

Venus in Signs

Venus in Aries (Venus/Mars/1st)
Favorable: Charming; likeable; love of life; energetic; passionate; youthful
Unfavorable: Inconsiderate; sweet-talker; conflicts in love; undependable; intimate too quickly

Venus in Taurus (Venus/Venus/2nd)
Favorable: Artistic; steady in love; love of tradition; conservative; prosperity
Unfavorable: Indulgent; too much leisure; possessive; too conservative in romantic ideals

Venus in Gemini (Venus/Mercury/3rd)
Favorable: Versatile; creative flair; needs changes; love of reading and writing; charming
Unfavorable: Divided in love; fickle; sense of duality in romance; hard to choose

Venus in Cancer (Venus/Moon/4th)
Favorable: Loving; treats others like family; love of family; imaginative; creative
Unfavorable: Unhappiness in love and family; too indulgent; reckless with blessings

Venus in Leo (Venus/Sun/5th)
Favorable: Elegant; charismatic; self-assured; appealing; good romance and love
Unfavorable: Haughty; vain; overconfident; domineering partners; overspends

Venus in Virgo (Venus/Mercury/6th)
Favorable: Spiritual views on love; conservative ideals; idealistic love and romance
Unfavorable: Trouble pleasing partners; dissatisfied; difficulties in love; inelegant; cold

Venus in Libra (Venus/Venus/7th)
Favorable: Accommodating; gracious; prosperous; good dealings; artistic; harmonious
Unfavorable: Lack of initiative; overconfident; disinterest in partners; spendthrift; vain

Venus in Scorpio (Venus/Mars/8th)

Favorable: Energetic; passionate; alluring; full of vigor; artistic; fascinating

Unfavorable: Undependable in love; scandals; intimate quickly; submissive; mistreatment

Venus in Sagittarius (Venus/Jupiter/9th)

Favorable: Love of freedom and justice; free-spirited; artistic; humanitarian; prosperous mates

Unfavorable: Lack of direction or planning; too optimistic; rebellious; defiant

Venus in Capricorn (Venus/Saturn/10th)

Favorable: Loyal; dedicated; faithful; love of traditions; simple approach

Unfavorable: Lack of prosperity; remorseful; restrictions or delays in love; dispirited

Venus in Aquarius (Venus/Saturn/11th)

Favorable: Extraordinary relationships; accepting in love; faithful; loves the unusual; innovative

Unfavorable: Weird love or romances; restrictions in love; lack of self-esteem; low partners

Venus in Pisces (Venus/Venus/12th)

Favorable: Prosperity; artistic; love of philosophy and spirituality; elegance; full of love

Unfavorable: Losses through love; poor or noncontributing partners; lack of prosperity

Shani (Saturn) planetary yantra.

Saturn in Signs

Saturn in Aries (Saturn/Mars/1st)
Favorable: Dynamic action; focused efforts; gains over time; high energy
Unfavorable: Too impatient; aggressive; inconsiderate; cruel; ruthless; depressed; hyper

Saturn in Taurus (Saturn/Mars/2nd)

Favorable: Traditional paths to wealth; wealth later in life; focused; conservative approach

Unfavorable: Frustrated finances and love; slow growth; doesn't acquire much; lack of beauty

Saturn in Gemini (Saturn/Mercury/3rd)

Favorable: Focused mind; convincing speaker; mechanical approach; traditional creativity

Unfavorable: Obsessed; overcommitted; lack of creativity; dull; trouble communicating

Saturn in Cancer (Saturn/Moon/4th)

Favorable: Steady emotions; dependable; solid family; traditional home life

Unfavorable: Obstinate; restricted emotions; troubles in family; lack of love; unexpressive

Saturn in Leo (Saturn/Sun/5th)

Favorable: Diligent; finds a way to make it work; responsible leader; traditional approach

Unfavorable: Domineering; micromanages; lack of charisma; too controlled; overworks

Saturn in Virgo (Saturn/Mercury/6th)

Favorable: Good planner and organizer; handles the details; focused; orderly; systematic

Unfavorable: Too focused on small detail; obsessive-compulsive; stuck mentality; risk averse

Saturn in Libra (Saturn/Venus/7th)
Favorable: Steady in love; smart; prosperous over time; things tend to work out; good dealings
Unfavorable: Overly focused on pleasure; restricted love; dissatisfaction

Saturn in Scorpio (Saturn/Mars/8th)
Favorable: Executive energy; vigorous; fast and steady; acts within correct time frame
Unfavorable: Aggressive; antagonistic; ruthless; intolerant; on edge; tired out; erratic

Saturn in Sagittarius (Saturn/Jupiter/9th)
Favorable: Ethical; legal disposition; makes a convincing case; brings justice; traditional
Unfavorable: Restricted expansion; lack of prosperity; legal troubles; unjust

Saturn in Capricorn (Saturn/Saturn/10th)
Favorable: Focused; structured; success over time; steady; dependable
Unfavorable: Self-centered; stuck; not trustworthy; obstacles and delays; goes too slowly

Saturn in Aquarius (Saturn/Saturn/11th)
Favorable: Steady progress through innovation and standards; does what's needed; traditional

Unfavorable: Restricted by unusual ideas; misalignment with peers; outcaste; low self-worth

Saturn in Pisces (Saturn/Jupiter/12th)

Favorable: Benefits from retreats; good spirituality; seeks liberation; steady; helpful advisor

Unfavorable: Gets wrong guru or advice; slow progress; pessimistic; low finances

Rahu (North Node of the Moon) planetary yantra.

Rahu in Signs

Rahu in Aries (Rahu/Mars/1st)
Favorable: Motivated; foreign and/or innovative approaches; energetic; enthusiastic
Unfavorable: Confused actions; deceptive; too pushy; toxins in body; foreign troubles

Rahu in Taurus (Rahu/Venus/2nd)

Favorable: Unusual love; innovative acquisition; unique possessions; follows odd traditions

Unfavorable: Stubborn; confusion in love or gender identity; financial loss through foreigners

Rahu in Gemini (Rahu/Mercury/3rd)

Favorable: Innovative thinking; thinks "outside the box"; takes unusual approaches; ingenious

Unfavorable: Confused; misunderstood; crooked thinking; mental problems; misleading speech

Rahu in Cancer (Rahu/Moon/4th)

Favorable: Comfortable in foreign situations; stays grounded in confused times; innovative

Unfavorable: Emotional problems; confusions in family; doubtful; inappropriate feelings

Rahu in Leo (Rahu/Sun/5th)

Favorable: Takes the lead in unclear situations; in control in foreign settings; exotic appeal

Unfavorable: Deceptive leadership; suspicious activities; oddly ostentatious; strange persona

Rahu in Virgo (Rahu/Mercury/6th)

Favorable: Innovative thinker; analysis removes confusion; takes novel approaches

Unfavorable: Confused; toxic thoughts; negative; mental problems

Rahu in Libra (Rahu/Venus/7th)

Favorable: Unconventional attitudes and actions in love; love of the foreign; exotic artistry

Unfavorable: Confusions in love; deceptive or confused partners; crooked dealings; unbalanced

Rahu in Scorpio (Rahu/Mars/8th)

Favorable: Investigative; reveals transcendental knowledge; uncovers secrets; detoxifies

Unfavorable: Confused or deceptive; uncaring; ruthless; too aggressive; trouble with extremes

Rahu in Sagittarius (Rahu/Jupiter/9th)

Favorable: Clears up ethical problems; counsels the confused; reveals the right course of action

Unfavorable: Misleading philosophies or ideas; swindler; worthless gimmicks; misrepresents

Rahu in Capricorn (Rahu/Saturn/10th)

Favorable: Innovative practicality; clears things up; bring unusual and innovative processes

Unfavorable: Creates confusion by staying with old ways; ruthless; deceptive; dishonest

Rahu in Aquarius (Rahu/Saturn/11th)

Favorable: Creates breakthroughs; innovative; avant-garde; helps foreigners and the confused

Unfavorable: Misleads the results of innovations; troubles in foreign locales; too strange

Rahu in Pisces (Rahu/Jupiter/12th)

Favorable: New Age spirituality; esoteric philosophy; clarifies ancient knowledge; modernizes

Unfavorable: Bogus spirituality; hypocrite; makes something appear more than it's worth

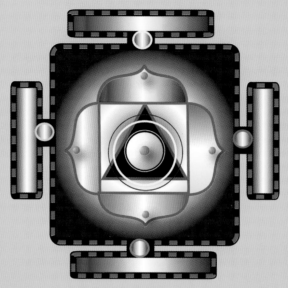

Ketu (South Node of the Moon) planetary yantra.

Ketu in Signs

Ketu in Aries (Ketu/Mars/1st)
Favorable: Flexible; adaptable; able to quickly change the course; innovator; early implementer
Unfavorable: Erratic; rash; inconsistent; sudden changes or surprises

Ketu in Taurus (Ketu/Venus/2nd)

Favorable: Accumulates spiritual things; helps others reorganize finances; adaptable speaker

Unfavorable: Inconsistent speech; erratic finances; irregular diet and eating; unreliable

Ketu in Gemini (Ketu/Mercury/3rd)

Favorable: Creative speaker, writer, and thinker; innovative communications or seminars

Unfavorable: Unpredictable; inconsistent way of communicating; too much change; chaotic

Ketu in Cancer (Ketu/Moon/4th)

Favorable: Spiritual feelings; intuitive; instinctive; innovative educator; spiritual teacher

Unfavorable: Emotionally undependable; broken home; uneven home life; hard to settle down

Ketu in Leo (Ketu/Sun/5th)

Favorable: Creative leadership; open-minded personality; spiritual disposition

Unfavorable: Lack of material interest; inconsistent approach; ups and downs with health

Ketu in Virgo (Ketu/Mercury/6th)

Favorable: Creative; breakthrough thinking; sees in a different light; intuitive

Unfavorable: Unreliable; loses interest quickly; hesitates; inconsistent responses to others

Ketu in Libra (Ketu/Venus/7th)

Favorable: Adaptable in love; flexible with partners; spiritual artistry; adaptable in business

Unfavorable: Undependable in love; dissatisfied; broken partnerships; sudden surprises in love

Ketu in Scorpio (Ketu/Mars/8th)

Favorable: Investigates the unknown; researcher; brings quick changes; adaptable

Unfavorable: Angry; expectations not met; surprising changes; uneven activity

Ketu in Sagittarius (Ketu/Jupiter/9th)

Favorable: Deals with changes through innate wisdom; spiritual knower; learns through change

Unfavorable: Changes too much and too quickly; erratic finances; undependable counselors

Ketu in Capricorn (Ketu/Saturn/10th)

Favorable: Entrepreneur; change agent; gains through speculation and agility in business

Unfavorable: Stability followed by sudden changes; ups and downs; hard to progress

Ketu in Aquarius (Ketu/Saturn/11th)

Favorable: Modernizes; repurposes business structures; gives a structure to the mystical

Unfavorable: Too innovative without enough standards; bizarre changes; chaotic; feels lost

Ketu in Pisces (Ketu/Jupiter/12th)

Favorable: Spiritual; wise; adaptable; innovative; brings old knowledge into modern settings

Unfavorable: Disconnected; difficult to make progress; sudden financial losses; unsuccessful

Just as the position of a planet in a sign will take on the characteristics of the ruler of the sign and its natural location in the zodiac, the planets in houses behave in a somewhat similar fashion. We can look at a planet in a house as being influenced by the natural zodiac sign represented by that house and that sign's natural ruler. For example, Sun in the first house will carry influences similar to a Sun/Mars combination and the position of the Sun in Aries (which is ruled by Mars). Combine the keywords to form simple interpretive statements.

Surya, graha deity for the Sun.

Sun in Houses

Sun in 1st House (Sun/Mars/Aries)
Favorable: Energetic; competitive; executive decisions; good vitality; confident
Unfavorable: Arrogant; too competitive; aggressive; angry; impatient; overconfident

Sun in 2nd House (Sun/Venus/Taurus)
Favorable: Persistent; influential and charming; good voice; accumulates wealth; healthy diet
Unfavorable: Extravagant; doesn't save; boastful; too loud or forceful; takes stimulants

Sun in 3rd House (Sun/Mercury/Gemini)
Favorable: Courageous; speaker/writer; outstanding actions; determined; prominent; inspiring
Unfavorable: Antagonistic; too insistent; unreliable; conflicting; reckless

Sun in 4th House (Sun/Moon/Cancer)
Favorable: Educator; caring; good home and fixed assets
Unfavorable: Emotional turmoil; unhappy; conflicts with authorities; in a rush

Sun in 5th House (Sun/Sun/Leo)
Favorable: Leader; good discrimination; benefits from children; romantic; sporty; speculative
Unfavorable: Immature; trouble with children; decides too fast; bad speculation; poor business

Sun in 6th House (Sun/Mercury/Virgo)

Favorable: Warrior; defeats opponents; heals quickly; strategic; protective; bold; witty

Unfavorable: Speedy; can't slow down; too aggressive; thief; combative; too clever

Sun in 7th House (Sun/Venus/Libra)

Favorable: Good dealings; strong partnerships; charming; mediator; sees all sides

Unfavorable: Impatient with partners; self-seeking; manipulative; deceptive; schemer

Sun in 8th House (Sun/Mars/Scorpio)

Favorable: Good support; windfalls; vital; investigative; spiritual yet sensual; secret success

Unfavorable: Too secretive; scandals; not trustworthy; too sensual; taken advantage of; angry

Sun in 9th House (Sun/Jupiter/Sagittarius)

Favorable: Fortunate; spiritual or ethical leader; gets high knowledge; has grace; full of merit

Unfavorable: Unlucky; trouble with authorities; hard travels; too fast; misses out; irreligious

Sun in 10th House (Sun/Saturn/Capricorn)

Favorable: Successful career; good reputation; personal power; respected; takes action

Unfavorable: Career problems; conflicts with authorities; lack of power; disrespected; angry

Sun in 11th House (Sun/Saturn/Aquarius)

Favorable: Good profits and cash flow; helpful friends and allies; benefits from elder sibling

Unfavorable: Cash-flow problems; small gains; lack of friends; poor networker

Sun in 12th House (Sun/Jupiter/Pisces)

Favorable: Spiritual seeker; benefits from seclusion; helps others get liberated; gains overseas

Unfavorable: Losses through lack of attention; timing is off; disinterested; too sensual; loner

Chandra, graha deity for the Moon.

Moon in Houses

Moon in 1st House (Moon/Mars/Aries)

Favorable: Royal disposition; compassionate; nurturing; encouraging; emotionally rich

Unfavorable: Vacillates; taken advantage of; can't disengage; hypersensitive; scattered emotions

Moon in 2nd House (Moon/Venus/Taurus)

Favorable: Accumulates wealth; collector; effective speech; gracious; good food; focused

Unfavorable: Indulgent; lack of application; wealth fluctuates; incorrect diet; poor speech

Moon in 3rd House (Moon/Mercury/Gemini)

Favorable: Fun loving; adventurous; communicator; writer; speaker; imaginative; determined

Unfavorable: Inconsistent effort; too scattered; lackadaisical; careless; naive

Moon in 4th House (Moon/Moon/Cancer)

Favorable: Intuitive; teacher; counselor; emotional depth; motherly; gets comforts of home

Unfavorable: Lack of emotional continuity; family trouble; lonely; no steady home; gullible

Moon in 5th House (Moon/Sun/Leo)

Favorable: Good-humored; romantic; intuitive discrimination; meditative; business success

Unfavorable: Gambler; restless; indiscriminate; unbalanced children; trouble meditating

Moon in 6th House (Moon/Mercury/Virgo)

Favorable: Healer; protector; defender; good service provider; instinctive; shrewd; active

Unfavorable: Agitated; conflicting; picky; poor service; trouble with servants, illnesses

Moon in 7th House (Moon/Venus/Libra)

Favorable: Passionate; loving; eager; lively partner

Unfavorable: Capricious; too ardent; inconsistent with partners; unreliable dealings

Moon in 8th House (Moon/Mars/Scorpio)

Favorable: Insightful; investigative; vital; gains support of others; transcendental; mystic

Unfavorable: Worried; alone; isolated; poor self-promotion; victim; lack of support; illnesses

Moon in 9th House (Moon/Jupiter/Sagittarius)

Favorable: Lucky; high knowledge; good ethics; popular; prosperous; benefits in travel

Unfavorable: Inconsistent fortune; too open to charlatans; ethical dilemmas; weak from travel

Moon in 10th House (Moon/Saturn/Capricorn)

Favorable: Gracious; good reputation; nurtures others; emotional depth; admired; good finances

Unfavorable: Scattered career success; indecisive; fluctuating life; trouble with emotions at work

Moon in 11th House (Moon/Saturn/Aquarius)

Favorable: Good cash flow; emotional ties with friends and allies; imaginative; opportunities

Unfavorable: Undependable with friends; unsteady alliances; infrequent gains and opportunity

Moon in 12th House (Moon/Jupiter/Pisces)

Favorable: Spiritually advanced; open; releasing; comforting; happy with what they have

Unfavorable: Troubled; stays in relationships too long; idealistic in love; victim; no focus; lost

Mangala, graha deity for Mars.

MARS IN HOUSES

Mars in 1st House (Mars/Mars/Aries)

Favorable: Energetic; enthusiastic; warrior; wholehearted approach; quick action; in the moment

Unfavorable: Heated; erratic; intolerant; impulsive; unsympathetic; reckless; fanatical; cruel

Mars in 2nd House (Mars/Mars/Taurus)

Favorable: Motivational speaker; popular; makes money quickly; delightful

Unfavorable: Harsh speech; defiant; compulsive spending; misleading; lack of focus; bad food

Mars in 3rd House (Mars/Mercury/Gemini)

Favorable: Adventurous; courageous; good comrade; writer; speaker; sales; persuasive

Unfavorable: Audacious; out of control; manipulative; unbelievable; irresponsible; too excited

Mars in 4th House (Mars/Moon/Cancer)

Favorable: Passionate; fervent feelings; quick to respond; faces up to problems

Unfavorable: Argumentative; hot temper; demanding; uncomfortable; impatient; rough emotions

Mars in 5th House (Mars/Sun/Leo)

Favorable: Appealing; decisive; protective; principled; honorable; exuberant; sporty

Unfavorable: Devious; corruptible; speedy mind; decides abruptly; too risky; fast intimacy

Mars in 6th House (Mars/Mercury/Virgo)
Favorable: Capable; courageous; acts fast; warrior; defender; healer; improver; beats opponents
Unfavorable: Defensive; unlawful; accidents/injuries; too rushed; vindictive; indebted; enemies

Mars in 7th House (Mars/Venus/Libra)
Favorable: Charismatic; quick business deals; affectionate; cheering; demonstrates love
Unfavorable: Partnership conflicts; disagreeable; too passionate; jealous; bad deals

Mars in 8th House (Mars/Mars/Scorpio)
Favorable: Gets support quickly; investigative; vigorous; competitive; active mystic
Unfavorable: Fierce; unpredictable; treacherous; unreliable; hotheaded; serious illness

Mars in 9th House (Mars/Jupiter/Sagittarius)
Favorable: Fast fortunes; energetic counselor; benefits from travel; quick to defend
Unfavorable: Immoral; bad conduct; sudden misfortunes; disrespects honorable people

Mars in 10th House (Mars/Saturn/Capricorn)

Favorable: Active career; executive ability; popular; clever; decisive; powerful leader

Unfavorable: Broken career; impulsive; mistakes; inaccurate; oversights; overspends

Mars in 11th House (Mars/Saturn/Aquarius)

Favorable: Good profits and cash flow; networker; good alliances and friends; quick profits

Unfavorable: Sporadic cash flow; mismanages; loss of opportunity; conflicts with friends

Mars in 12th House (Mars/Jupiter/Pisces)

Favorable: Rapid evolution; freedom fighter; liberator; inspirational; enthusiastic motivator

Unfavorable: Overspending; wasteful; too aggressive; lack of application; fines; punishment

Budha, graha deity for Mercury.

Mercury in Houses

Mercury in 1st House (Mercury/Mars/Aries)

Favorable: Clever; witty; analytical; systematic approach; logical; efficient; knowledgeable

Unfavorable: Indecisive; too changeable; lacks staying power; spread out too much

Mercury in 2nd House (Mercury/Venus/Taurus)

Favorable: Planner; speaker; strategic; analytical; clever investments

Unfavorable: Devious; schemer; too talkative; hesitates; inattention to finances

Mercury in 3rd House (Mercury/Mercury/Gemini)

Favorable: Tactical; technical; writer; lecturer; seminar speaker; communicator; musician; sales

Unfavorable: Tricky; unreliable speech; misrepresents; poor communicator; too talkative

Mercury in 4th House (Mercury/Moon/Cancer)

Favorable: Knowledgeable; imaginative; keeps learning; academic skills; cheerful

Unfavorable: Intellect dominates emotions; confused; unfeeling; mechanical

Mercury in 5th House (Mercury/Sun/Leo)

Favorable: Discriminating; perceptive; skilled meditator; insightful; observant; business skill

Unfavorable: Too selective; critical; pessimistic; unromantic; skeptical; thinks too much

Mercury in 6th House (Mercury/Mercury/Virgo)

Favorable: Outwits opposition; strategic; offers improvements to others; a fixer; survivor

Unfavorable: Argumentative; contrarian; dominating; troubled mind

Mercury in 7th House (Mercury/Venus/Libra)

Favorable: Composed in business; clever dealings; diplomatic; analytical transactions

Unfavorable: Distant to partners; dispassionate; lack of artistry; aloof; mechanical

Mercury in 8th House (Mercury/Mars/Scorpio)

Favorable: Diagnostician; investigator; clever planner/strategist; transcendental thoughts

Unfavorable: Mental problems; volatile; submissive; confused; deceptive; misunderstands; naive

Mercury in 9th House (Mercury/Jupiter/Sagittarius)

Favorable: Seeks higher knowledge; intellectual; advocate for justice; good fortune; writer

Unfavorable: Inconsistent or changeable philosophies; challenges teachers; deceptive teachings

Mercury in 10th House (Mercury/Saturn/Capricorn)

Favorable: Mental approach; cheerful; encouraging; analytical skills; teacher; inventor

Unfavorable: Too clever; deceptive; misrepresents the facts; manipulates data; fragmented

Mercury in 11th House (Mercury/Saturn/Aquarius)
Favorable: Business profits; good planning; clever cash flow; friendly; forms alliances
Unfavorable: Questions their friends and allies; deceptive plans; overanalyzes; confused

Mercury in 12th House (Mercury/Jupiter/Pisces)
Favorable: Spiritual intellect; philosophic insights; meditative; success in seclusion
Unfavorable: Penny-pinching creates losses; confused philosophies; tries too hard for moksha

Guru, graha deity for Jupiter.

Jupiter in Houses

Jupiter in 1st House (Jupiter/Mars/Aries)

Favorable: Confident; belief in positive outcomes; comforting; gracious; generous; expansive

Unfavorable: Slow to react to opportunities; unmindful; overindulges; lethargic

Jupiter in 2nd House (Jupiter/Venus/Taurus)

Favorable: Financial growth and accumulation; reassuring; good speech; comforting; good food

Unfavorable: Wasteful; uneconomical; lack of focus and application; meager finances; bad food

Jupiter in 3rd House (Jupiter/Mercury/Gemini)

Favorable: Expands through adventure; clever speaker/writer; communicator; persuasive; artistic

Unfavorable: Lack of initiative; unenthusiastic; irresolute; cowardly; careless conversations

Jupiter in 4th House (Jupiter/Moon/Cancer)

Favorable: Educated; instructs and informs others; knowledgeable; comforting; prosperous

Unfavorable: Unmotivated; overconfident; indulgent; careless; lack of real comforts

Jupiter in 5th House (Jupiter/Sun/Leo)

Favorable: Intelligent; philosophic; spiritual; business success; playful; positive; entertaining

Unfavorable: Careless discrimination; overindulges in pleasure and romance; immature; naive

Jupiter in 6th House (Jupiter/Mercury/Virgo)
Favorable: Legal skills; advocate for the weak; clever strategist; self-improvement expert
Unfavorable: Excessive spending; loss through inattention; unsteady growth; defenseless

Jupiter in 7th House (Jupiter/Venus/Libra)
Favorable: Grows through partners; business expands; good dealings; counselor; negotiator
Unfavorable: Lack of attention on partners; self-seeking; lazy; loss through misdealings

Jupiter in 8th House (Jupiter/Mars/Scorpio)
Favorable: Gets other people's money and support; spiritual growth; positive mystic; comforts
Unfavorable: Excessive behaviors; wastes resources; lack of support; ineffective; weak; lazy

Jupiter in 9th House (Jupiter/Jupiter/Sagittarius)
Favorable: Philosophical; guru; counselor; ethical; good fortune; higher education; generous
Unfavorable: Lacks good guru or mentor; wrong philosophies; fortunes dissipate; fanatic

Jupiter in 10th House (Jupiter/Saturn/Capricorn)

Favorable: Good career; counselor; teacher; advisor; high status and reputation; good knowledge

Unfavorable: Lack of application to career; inattentive to impacts on reputation; undirected

Jupiter in 11th House (Jupiter/Saturn/Aquarius)

Favorable: Good profits and cash flow; grows through friends and alliances; lots of opportunities

Unfavorable: Careless with money; inattentive to maintaining friendships; wastes opportunities

Jupiter in 12th House (Jupiter/Jupiter/Pisces)

Favorable: Liberated; expansive life; benefits from ashrams, hospitals, places of confinement

Unfavorable: Losses through lack of attention; indulgent; idle; overgenerous; too lenient

Shukra, graha deity for Venus.

Venus in Houses

Venus in 1st House (Venus/Mars/Aries)

Favorable: Charming; gracious; artistic; refined; love of beauty and art; appealing; prosperous

Unfavorable: Unresponsive; listless; extravagant; lack of effort; inelegant

Venus in 2nd House (Venus/Venus/Taurus)

Favorable: Prosperous; refined speech; good acquisitions; fine food and comforts; flourishes

Unfavorable: Uninspiring; vain; manipulative speech; uneventful life; lack of enjoyment

Venus in 3rd House (Venus/Mercury/Gemini)

Favorable: Creative; progressive; love of music and art; expressive; communicative

Unfavorable: Unaccomplished; lack of determination; low self-expression; timid; coy

Venus in 4th House (Venus/Moon/Cancer)

Favorable: Comfortable life; prosperous; reassuring; luxurious; thrives well; good assets

Unfavorable: Too lavish a lifestyle; not supportive; lethargic; self-seeking

Venus in 5th House (Venus/Sun/Leo)

Favorable: Charismatic; inspiring; romantic; congenial; comfortable spirituality

Unfavorable: Impractical; idealistic in business and love; too fancy; lack of romance

Venus in 6th House (Venus/Mercury/Virgo)
Favorable: Fights for what they love; heals wounded love; concerned; compassionate
Unfavorable: Friction and losses in love; lack of smoothness; expectations are too high

Venus in 7th House (Venus/Venus/Libra)
Favorable: Good mates; refined business; elegant dealings and interactions; positive exchanges
Unfavorable: Overindulgence in pleasure; ineffective partners; legal problems; bad partners

Venus in 8th House (Venus/Mars/Scorpio)
Favorable: Sexual vitality; energized by art and beauty; support by females; prospers
Unfavorable: Sexual difficulties; lack of beauty and refinement; not prosperous; unsophisticated

Venus in 9th House (Venus/Jupiter/Sagittarius)
Favorable: Life of blessings and beauty; ethical; cordial; fortune via females; fortunate, artful
Unfavorable: Careless; losses through lack of effort; trouble with females; lack of beauty and art

Venus in 10th House (Venus/Saturn/Capricorn)
Favorable: Career related to beauty, art, elegance; works in law; stylish; good reputation

Unfavorable: Trouble through women; lack of effort; not artful; uses deceit to get ahead

Venus in 11th House (Venus/Saturn/Aquarius)
Favorable: Good cash flow; fortune via friends and alliances; profits through women and art
Unfavorable: Loss of profits through women; lack of refinement; unattractive to supporters

Venus in 12th House (Venus/Jupiter/Pisces)
Favorable: Sensuous; tantric skills; spiritual artistry; devoted to love and spiritual growth
Unfavorable: Lack of application; big expenditures; inefficient; sexual troubles; too generous

Shani, graha deity for Saturn.

Saturn in Houses

Saturn in 1st House (Saturn/Mars/Aries)
Favorable: Patient; focused; methodical; astute; success over time; conservative
Unfavorable: Unclean habits; unscrupulous; too cunning; lack of attention; frustrated

Saturn in 2nd House (Saturn/Venus/Taurus)
Favorable: Focused study and attention; gains over time; careful speech; traditional
Unfavorable: Lack of wealth; doesn't speak out; dishonest; eating disorders

Saturn in 3rd House (Saturn/Mercury/Gemini)
Favorable: Determined application; steady efforts; conservative speaker/writer
Unfavorable: Risk averse; problems with siblings and neighbors; meek; blocked efforts

Saturn in 4th House (Saturn/Moon/Cancer)
Favorable: Learns steadily; emotions strengthen over time; traditionalist; careful
Unfavorable: Frustrated; discouraged; unhappy; stuck; pessimistic; lack of comforts

Saturn in 5th House (Saturn/Sun/Leo)
Favorable: Steady intellect; sound reasoning; traditional spiritual techniques; sound business
Unfavorable: Can't decide; dull; lack of discrimination; negative; unromantic; deceptive

Saturn in 6th House (Saturn/Mercury/Virgo)

Favorable: Outstrategizes opponents; protective; disciplined; regulates others; provides service

Unfavorable: Misplaced loyalties; stays involved too long; overworks; trapped; debts

Saturn in 7th House (Saturn/Venus/Libra)

Favorable: Devoted; faithful; traditional relationships; conservative business deals

Unfavorable: Delays or obstructions in relationships; commits late; dispassionate

Saturn in 8th House (Saturn/Mars/Scorpio)

Favorable: Discovers ancient knowledge; more support over time; endurance; survivor

Unfavorable: Victim; unsupported; obstructed; cruel; hindrances; controlling; ill health

Saturn in 9th House (Saturn/Jupiter/Sagittarius)

Favorable: Advocate for justice and traditions; prosperity builds up; steady fortune

Unfavorable: Conforming; bad luck; spiritual obstructions; unethical; on the run

Saturn in 10th House (Saturn/Saturn/Capricorn)

Favorable: Steady, conservative career; traditional values; conservative reputation; dependable

Unfavorable: Career encounters setbacks and delays; negative or dull reputation; selfish

Saturn in 11th House (Saturn/Saturn/Aquarius)

Favorable: Steady gains through dependable friends and allies; influential; cash flow grows

Unfavorable: Lack of opportunities; undependable friends; poor alliances; meager cash flow

Saturn in 12th House (Saturn/Jupiter/Pisces)

Favorable: Spiritual simplicity; liberation comes over time; joy in seclusion

Unfavorable: Dispassionate; lack of focus; doesn't care enough; stuck; losses; loner

Rahu, graha deity for the North Node of the Moon.

Rahu in Houses

Rahu in 1st House (Rahu/Mars/Aries)
Favorable: Finds a way to make it work; clarifies the path ahead; industrious; overcomes
Unfavorable: Fear of failing; confused; lack of goals; irritating; pushy; toxic; worrisome

Rahu in 2nd House (Rahu/Venus/Taurus)
Favorable: Benefits from face-to-face conversations; clever income; clarifies approaches
Unfavorable: Defective speech; dishonest; gullible; unscrupulous; suspicious income

Rahu in 3rd House (Rahu/Mercury/Gemini)
Favorable: Courage to take a novel approach; success with foreigners; adventuresome
Unfavorable: Misleading; confused efforts; ambiguous approach; hostile; too determined

Rahu in 4th House (Rahu/Moon/Cancer)
Favorable: Innovative perspectives; creative feelings; prospers with the unknown
Unfavorable: Frightens easily; afraid to commit; fearful; bewildered; undependable; hurt

Rahu in 5th House (Rahu/Sun/Leo)
Favorable: Clarifies illusions and misconceptions; success in foreign locales; handles confusion

Unfavorable: Not to be trusted; manipulates to their advantage; indecisive; tricky; false guru

Rahu in 6th House (Rahu/Mercury/Leo)
Favorable: Outsmarts opponents; clever planner; makes it happen; healer; triumphs
Unfavorable: Misunderstandings; feels estranged; unusual illnesses and accidents; sneaky

Rahu in 7th House (Rahu/Venus/Libra)
Favorable: Success with foreign partners and locales; clarifies business processes; succeeds
Unfavorable: Unfaithful; deceptive partners; lack of commitment; confused dealings

Rahu in 8th House (Rahu/Mars/Scorpio)
Favorable: Investigative; innovative researcher; transforms others through improving and purifying them; unusual windfalls
Unfavorable: Poor health; odd diseases; lacks support; betrayed; scandals; bad treatment: spy; thief

Rahu in 9th House (Rahu/Jupiter/Sagittarius)
Favorable: Successful; triumphant; conquering; unusual luck; prevails; not afraid of unknown
Unfavorable: Confusion with authorities; deception with guru; trouble with travels; unethical

Rahu in 10th House (Rahu/Saturn/Capricorn)

Favorable: Success in innovative pursuits; clarifies and overcomes problems; career prevails

Unfavorable: Confusion in career; uncertain of purpose; deceptive practices; bad reputation

Rahu in 11th House (Rahu/Saturn/Aquarius)

Favorable: Profits through innovation and foreign pursuits; ingenius friends and allies

Unfavorable: Lack of clarity hurts cash flow; deceptive or confused friends and allies

Rahu in 12th House (Rahu/Jupiter/Pisces)

Favorable: Remarkable spiritual path; success in foreign locales; gains enlightenment

Unfavorable: Unusual or unexpected hindrances; losses; confusion prevails; toxic problems

Ketu, graha deity for the South Node of the Moon.

Ketu in Houses

Ketu in 1st House (Ketu/Mars/Aries)

Favorable: Unexpected benefits; surprising growth; innovative disposition; lots of changes

Unfavorable: Desire for change brings chaos; inconstancy slows growth; bored; unfocused

Ketu in 2nd House (Ketu/Venus/Taurus)

Favorable: Reorganization brings new development; surprising income; creative speech

Unfavorable: Inconsistent; doesn't keep word; financial chaos; erratic diet; lack of focus

Ketu in 3rd House (Ketu/Mercury/Gemini)

Favorable: Surprising changes create growth; adaptable; mystical adventures; creative

Unfavorable: Lack of consistency and effort; broken communication; erratic thinking

Ketu in 4th House (Ketu/Moon/Cancer)

Favorable: Unpredictable circumstances strengthen feelings; flexible; instinctive; intuitive

Unfavorable: Erratic emotions; changes in home; lack of foundations; frequent change of mind

Ketu in 5th House (Ketu/Sun/Leo)

Favorable: Creative; adaptable; nimble; reorganizes well; business transformer; mystic

Unfavorable: Indecisive; lack of discrimination; perplexed; fraudulent; unreliable; gullible

Ketu in 6th House (Ketu/Mercury/Virgo)

Favorable: Transformative; healer; uncovers hidden meaning and mysteries; change agent

Unfavorable: Odd imaginings; fearful dreams; vulnerable to attack; shocking surprises

Ketu in 7th House (Ketu/Venus/Libra)

Favorable: Accommodating; flexible; allowing; spiritual partners; creative dealings

Unfavorable: Insecure or unstable relationships; cheating; inconstant commitments

Ketu in 8th House (Ketu/Mars/Scorpio)

Favorable: Intuitive; instinctual; rarified perceptions; spiritual healer; investigates mysteries

Unfavorable: Erratic health; difficult-to-diagnose disease; worried; false imaginations; changeable

Ketu in 9th House (Ketu/Jupiter/Sagittarius)

Favorable: Spiritual outlooks; mystical pilgrimages; studies many philosophies

Unfavorable: Lack of consistency; skeptical; seeks too many paths; unreliable guru

Ketu in 10th House (Ketu/Saturn/Capricorn)

Favorable: Innovative; seeks change; spiritual pursuits dominate career; many careers

Unfavorable: Joins a cult; inconsistent; erratic career status; surprises hurt reputation

Ketu in 11th House (Ketu/Saturn/Aquarius)

Favorable: Adaptability sustains cash flow; innovative and spiritual friends and allies

Unfavorable: Incomplete profits; erratic pursuit of opportunities; unreliable friends

Ketu in 12th House (Ketu/Jupiter/Pisces)

Favorable: Seeks enlightenment; spiritual pilgrimages; life in seclusion; humanitarian

Unfavorable: Lack of direction causes loss; erratic pursuit of spirituality; inconstancy

Yogas and Planetary Combinations

One of the distinctions of Vedic astrology is in how it keeps track of special combinations of planets, which are called a *yoga,* or "union." This yoga is not the stretching and health system called *hatha yoga,* but represents specific ways in which planets combine. Some planets join in ways that bring fortune and are called *dhana* (dah' nah), or "wealth," yogas; sometimes planets combine unfavorably as *aristha* (ah rish' tah), or "poverty," yogas, exposing the person to hardship and financial challenges. I've listed some types of yogas here.

Raja Yoga

Rulerships play an important part in the creation of yogas. Raja yoga is formed when the ruler of an angle or kendra house (1, 4, 7, 10) joins the ruler of a trine or trikona house (1, 5, 9). The first house, or Lagna, is considered both an angle and a trine and is an exception to the two-planet comment.

When two planets are combined in a raja yoga, it gives the person an increased ability to perform action at a higher level, such as that of a king (or executive in our modern world). The rest of the chart needs to be strong and favorable to fully support a raja yoga. An overall weak chart won't be able to fully sustain a raja yoga, although the yoga itself will help the chart.

Yoga Karaka

One simple yet important type of planetary yoga is called a *yoga karaka*. This indicates which specific planet will bring prosperity for specific rising signs. These yoga karakas are especially beneficial during their *dasa,* or "planetary periods" (more on dasas coming up).

Taurus and Libra ascendants have Saturn as the yoga karaka. For Taurus, Saturn rules the ninth (trine) house, and the tenth (angle) house. In Libra ascendants Saturn rules both the fourth (angle) and the fifth (trine).

Capricorn and Aquarius ascendants have Venus as the yoga karaka. For Capricorn, Venus rules the fifth (trine) and the tenth (angle). For Aquarius, Venus rules the fourth (angle) and ninth (trine).

Cancer and Leo ascendants have Mars as the yoga karaka. For Cancer, Mars rules the fifth (trine) and the tenth (angle). For Leo, Mars rules the fourth (angle) and the ninth (trine).

Dhana, or "Wealth," Yogas

This is another planetary yoga formed by house rulerships. *Dhana* means "wealth" and brings prosperity through the interconnection of the primary financial houses: 1, 2, 5, 9, and 11. For example, ruler of the first in the ninth, or second in the eleventh, and so on. Any combination of these houses will create dhana yoga, but the connections with the first house, our basic self, shows the most significant financial possibilities.

If you see dhana yogas in a chart, especially more than one, you should see some form of good success for that person—especially during the dasas, or transits, of the planets involved.

PANCHA MAHAPURUSHA
(PAHN' CHA MAH' HAH PUHR OO' SHAH) YOGAS

Mahapurusha yoga is created by the special position of a planet, rather than through a rulership connection. This yoga is formed when a planet—other than the Sun or Moon or the nodes—is in its own sign on an angle, or is exalted *and* is located in an angle. Some astrologers will look for these yogas from the Lagna and/or the Moon. These yogas create a lot of power for the planets involved. There are only five of these yogas in Vedic astrology. *Pancha* means "five," *maha* means "great," and *purusha* means "man." *Ruchaka* (roo chah' kah) yoga involves Mars; *Badhra* (bah' drah) yoga is created by Mercury; *Hamsa* (hahm' sah) yoga comes from Jupiter; *Malavya* (mah lah' vyah) and *Sasha* (sah' shah) yoga are generated by Saturn.

THE NAVAMSA

The creators of the Vedic astrology system divided the 360-degree wheel of the Sun—that is, the ecliptic—into 12 sections of 30 degrees each. This circular track forms the path the planets take within the 12 constellations of the zodiac. This is represented in the patterns written into the astrological map called the *horoscope,* or *rasi kundali,* in India.

The Vedic masters wanted to be able to get more resolution out of the Vedic map, so they set up a process wherein each of the 30-degree signs were subdivided into smaller divisions. In addition to the rasi, which we would consider a division of one, we get 16 additional divisions, which is called *shodasa vargas* (sho dah' shah var' gahs), meaning "16 divisions."

The most famous of these 16, next to the rasi, is what is called the *navamsa* (nahv ahm' shah) *chart.* This *varga,* or "divi-

sional chart," takes the 30-degree rasi chart and breaks it down into nine (nav) smaller divisions (amsas). So we get nine sections in the rasis that are 3 degrees and 20 minutes of arc—that is, 3 degrees and 20 minutes out of the 360-degree circle of the zodiac. While it takes about two hours for a rasi sign to pass by the ascendant point, it only takes the 1/9th-smaller navamsa 13 minutes and 20 seconds of clock time to pass through the ascendant's gate.

Since there are 12 rasis and 9 navamsa divisions within each rasi, there are a total of 108 navamsa *padas,* or "feet." The navamsa takes 108 steps to walk around the zodiac.

The 27 nakshatras, along with the 12 signs of the zodiac.

The first navamsa in Aries starts with Aries, then the remaining signs get placed. Then Aries starts the count again, going in 12 planet-repeating sequences around the chart until it ends with Pisces. You'll notice this number, 108, appears as the number of nakshatra padas as well. So we get a numerical alignment between the divisions of the solar zodiac signs and those of the Moon signs, or nakshatras, which will be covered in the next chapter.

All Vedic astrology software programs calculate the navamsa, so there's no need to go through the math of it here. Functionally, the purpose of the navamsa chart is to provide further insight into the subtle and perhaps not yet expressed aspects of one's life. You look primarily at the rasi chart, but examination of the navamsa can give you additional information that you might not see otherwise. Some liken the rasi chart to the tree and the navamsa to its fruits.

Pisces	Aries	Taurus	Gemini
1 Cancer 2 Leo 3 Virgo 4 Libra 5 Scorpio 6 Sagittarius 7 Capricorn 8 Aquarius 9 Pisces	1 Aries 2 Taurus 3 Gemini 4 Cancer 5 Leo 6 Virgo 7 Libra 8 Scorpio 9 Sagittarius	1 Capricorn 2 Aquarius 3 Pisces 4 Aries 5 Taurus 6 Gemini 7 Cancer 8 Leo 9 Virgo	1 Libra 2 Scorpio 3 Sagittarius 4 Capricorn 5 Aquarius 6 Pisces 7 Aries 8 Taurus 9 Gemini

Aquarius (left):
1 Libra, 2 Scorpio, 3 Sagittarius, 4 Capricorn, 5 Aquarius, 6 Pisces, 7 Aries, 8 Taurus, 9 Gemini

Cancer (right):
1 Cancer, 2 Leo, 3 Virgo, 4 Libra, 5 Scorpio, 6 Sagittarius, 7 Capricorn, 8 Aquarius, 9 Pisces

Capricorn (left):
1 Capricorn, 2 Aquarius, 3 Pisces, 4 Aries, 5 Taurus, 6 Gemini, 7 Cancer, 8 Leo, 9 Virgo

Leo (right):
1 Aries, 2 Taurus, 3 Gemini, 4 Cancer, 5 Leo, 6 Virgo, 7 Libra, 8 Scorpio, 9 Sagittarius

Sagittarius	Scorpio	Libra	Virgo
1 Aries 2 Taurus 3 Gemini 4 Cancer 5 Leo 6 Virgo 7 Libra 8 Scorpio 9 Sagittarius	1 Cancer 2 Leo 3 Virgo 4 Libra 5 Scorpio 6 Sagittarius 7 Capricorn 8 Aquarius 9 Pisces	1 Libra 2 Scorpio 3 Sagittarius 4 Capricorn 5 Aquarius 6 Pisces 7 Aries 8 Taurus 9 Gemini	1 Capricorn 2 Aquarius 3 Pisces 4 Aries 5 Taurus 6 Gemini 7 Cancer 8 Leo 9 Virgo

The Navamsa Chart: The navamsa divides each sign into nine (nav) subsections called navamsa padas. The navamsa is said to give the "fruit" of the chart or subtle influences not seen in the rasi, or main birth chart, which some would liken to the "tree" of the chart.

Rahu, the North Node of the Moon.

CHAPTER SEVEN

THE 27 *NAKSHATRAS* OR "MOON SIGNS"

Benign to me be all those Lunar Mansions to
which the Moon as he moves doth honor.
— Atharvaveda Book 19, Hymn 8

We know the apparent path of the Sun, the ecliptic, is divided into 12 sections. These form the signs of the zodiac. In Vedic astrology, the zodiac is also subdivided into 27 nakshatras, or what some call Moon Signs, Lunar Mansions, or asterisms (a subconstellation). The nakshatras have a *yoga tara* (tah' rah), or "marker star" that helps identify each asterism's boundary location. Some researchers feel that the use of marker stars was the original method for locating planets and star groups before using the intersection of the Earth's equator and ecliptic as a starting point of the zodiac.

Each nakshatra covers 13 degrees and 20 minutes of the 360-degree solar zodiac. While the Sun stays about a month in each sign of the zodiac, the Moon stays in

Locating a nakshatra via a yoga tara, or "marker star."

each nakshatra for about a day. The passage of the Moon and the various planets are tracked as they move through each nakshatra. In the early days of Jyotish, the Vedic priests kept track of the Moon in the various nakshatras to identify appropriate days to perform religious rituals. Their purpose was to keep the energy of life positive and supportive with the forces of creative intelligence. Thus, reciprocally, the hope was that the elemental forces of nature would stay supportive of the population.

The location of your Moon at the time of your birth is called your *janma nakshatra* ("birth nakshatra"). Some people will also call this your "birth star." In the interpretation of a Vedic chart, we would want to examine the nakshatra the Moon occupies and the nakshatra occupied by the rising sign degree.

The information contained in the nakshatras expands on what we find in the rasi (birth chart). When you examine the current Vedic astrology literature translated into English, you'll find that there isn't as much information on nakshatras as there is on rasis. However, you can judge the favorable or unfavorable quality of a nakshatra in a fashion similar to judging a sign or house—that is, by the quality of the planets that aspect and occupy it. As always, the indications from the nakshatras have to be balanced against the indicators seen in the natal chart as a whole. Most likely the natal or rasi chart indications will dominate, but the nakshatra of the Moon and of the rising sign degree can give you a meaningful overtone about who you are.

Translation and Symbol: Each nakshatra has a specific translation from Sanskrit and is identified with a certain symbol. The meaning of these two things add descriptive character to each nakshatra.

Presiding Deity: Each person is identified in their chart by their Moon nakshatra, also called the *janma nakshatra*. The descriptions of the deity plays a role in defining the nature and temperament of a person. Knowing the personality and character of the nakshatra's deity gives us additional insight into a person's nature. It's interesting to note that while the nakshatras were originally considered star groups to mark the passage of the Moon in order to time rituals, the deities associated with the nakshatras are often representative of various forms or qualities of sunlight. In a higher sense, this light is also regarded as forms of the light of consciousness, calling to mind our earlier statements about the multiply layers of meaning of Vedic thought and its integrated nature.

Marker Star: Each nakshatra is traditionally identified by a marker star called a yoga tara, or "union star," which shows where one nakshatra joins another in the 27 asterisms or subconstellations of the nakshatra system of sky division. Some researchers will disagree as to which specific star is the fiducial or marker star. What I have listed on the following pages are what seem to be the choices made by the majority of Vedic researchers.

Dasa Planet: The dasas are special forecasting techniques of astrology to determine when the planets in the chart will manifest their influence at various ages in a person's life. Each dasa period follows a span and sequence of years, calculated from the position of the Moon in a persons chart, as located in a nakshatra. While the nakshatra is used to calculate the starting point of a person's 120-year dasa cycle, some astrologers also treat the planet ruling the nakshatra in the same fashion as they treat planets ruling signs. The software included with this book will calculate the dasas for you.

Right: Symbols of the 27 nakshatras and the 12 zodiac signs.

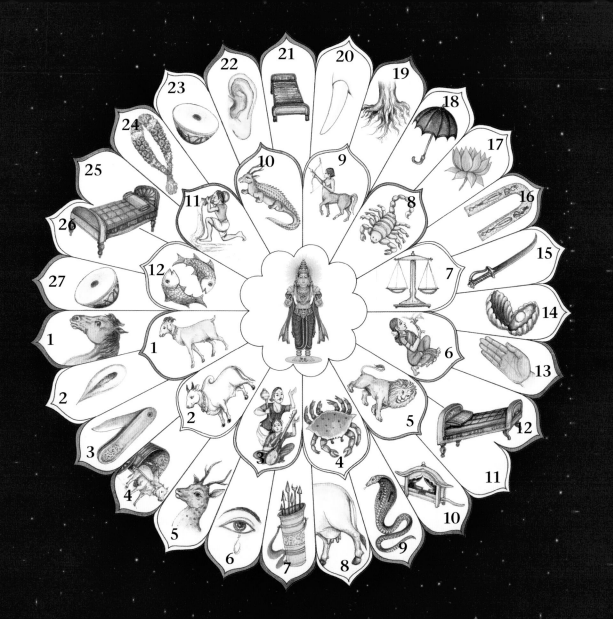

Ashwini #1
(ahsh win' nee)
Aries 0–00 to Aries 13–20

Translation: The horseman or horse harnessers
Symbol: Horse's head
Deity: Ashwini Kumars, Physicians of the Gods; some say Agni, the Fire God
Marker Star: α Alpha or β Beta Arietis (air ee eh' tis)
Dasa Planet: Ketu
Key Concept: Healing; dawn of new things; new beginnings; movement forward; miracles

Bharani #2
(bahr' on nee)
Aries 13–20 to Aries 26–40

Translation: The bearer (one who bears burdens)
Symbol: Yoni—sex organ, womb, point of origin
Deity: Yama, God of Control or Death
Marker Star: γ Gamma Arietis (air ee eh' tis)
Dasa Planet: Venus
Key Concept: Self-control; responsibility; gives birth to new things; burdens; struggling, hidden and obstructed life events

Krittika #3
(krih' tih kah)
Aries 26–40 to Taurus 10–00

Translation: The cutter
Symbol: Sharp weapon (razor or ax), flame
Deity: Agni, God of Fire and Light
Marker Star: η Eta Tauri (toh' ree) or Alcyone (al see' ohn)
Dasa Planet: Sun
Key Concept: Bright or sharp mind and body; ambitious; creative

Rohini #4
(roh hee' nee)
Taurus 10–00 to Taurus 23–20

Translation: The red one or the red deer
Symbol: Cart (ox drawn)
Deity: Brahma or Prajapati (prah jah' puh tee) the Creator
Marker Star: α Alpha Tauri (toh' ree) or Aldebaran (al deb' ah rahn)
Dasa Planet: Moon
Key Concept: Desire for growth and position of self and others

MRIGASHIRA #5
(mrig ah sheer' ah)
Taurus 23–20 to Gemini 6–40

Translation: Deer's head
Symbol: Head of a deer
Deity: Soma, the Moon; or Amrita (ahm' rih tah), the Ambrosia of the Gods
Marker Star: λ Lambda Orionis (oh ree ohn' us)
Dasa Planet: Mars
Key Concept: Taking the path to knowledge and enlightenment

ARDRA #6
(ar' drah)
Gemini 6–40 to Gemini 20–00

Translation: Teardrop or moisture (in the body)
Symbol: Teardrop or drop of moisture
Deity: Rudra (roo' drah) the Howler, Lord of Storms
Marker Star: α Orionis or Betelgeuse (bee' tuhl jooz)
Dasa Planet: Rahu
Key Concept: Removing or liberating oneself from tears and distress by properly applying one's self to the task (no sweating and straining)

PUNARVASU #7
(poo nar vah' soo)
Gemini 20–00 to Cancer 3–20

Translation: Repeating prosperity or brilliance, "good again"
Symbol: Quiver of arrows or an arrow
Deity: Aditi (ah dee' tee) the Boundless—a Sun Goddess indicating unlimited life
Marker Star: β Beta Geminorium (jem i noh' rum) or Pollox
Dasa Planet: Jupiter
Key Concept: A life of repeating prosperity and brilliance

PUSHYA #8
(poosh yah')
Cancer 3–20 to Cancer 16–40

Translation: Nourishing or a flower
Symbol: Udder of a cow, a flower
Deity: Brahmanaspati (brah mahn' ahs pah tee) or Brihaspati (bree hus' pah tee), Lord of Prayers
Marker Star: δ Delta Cancri (kan' kree)
Dasa Planet: Saturn
Key Concept: Being nourished in the fullness of life; abundance of life's bounty

ASLESHA #9
(ahsh lay' sha)
Cancer 16–40 to Leo 0–00

Translation: Entwiner (like a snake)
Symbol: Coiled serpent
Deity: Naga (nah' gah), a snake, Lord of Serpents
Marker Star: ε Epsilon Hydrae (high' dree)
Dasa Planet: Mercury
Key Concept: Removing obstructions to live an unbounded life

MAGHA #10
(mug' ha)
Leo 0–00 to Leo 13–20

Translation: The mighty one
Symbol: Palanquin, royal canopy
Deity: Pitris, a "father," the forefathers or ancestors said to dwell in the firmament or the atmosphere—the place between the earth and the heavens
Marker Star: α Alpha Leonis (lee' oh nis) or Regulus (rehg' yoo luhs)
Dasa Planet: Ketu
Key Concept: Being royal; leading; motivating; inspiring

Purvaphalguni #11
(pur vah pal' goo nee)
Leo 13–20 to Leo 26–40

Translation: Former red one or fig tree
Symbol: Front legs of a bed
Deity: Bhaga or "Fortune," or the "Dispenser" (some say the deity is Aryaman)
Marker Star: δ Delta Leonis
Dasa Planet: Venus
Key Concept: Keeping agreements; forming alliances; having the pleasure of interacting with and being a good host to others

Uttaraphalguni #12
(oo tah rah pal' goo nee)
Leo 26–40 to Virgo 10–00

Translation: Latter red one or fig tree
Symbol: Back legs of a bed
Deity: Aryaman the Companion, Lord of Hospitality (some say the deity is Bhaga or Aryaman-Bhaga together)
Marker Star: β Beta Leonis or Denebola (duh neb' oh lah)
Dasa Planet: Sun
Key Concept: Bringing things to fruition

HASTA #13
(hah stah')
Virgo 10–00 to Virgo 23–20

Translation: The hand or clenched fist
Symbol: Palm of the hand or a fist
Deity: Savitri (sah vee' tree) the Vivifier, the Sun as the stimulator of life
Marker Star: δ Delta Corvi (cohr' vee)
Dasa Planet: Moon
Key Concept: Indicates grasping power, both in acquiring money and knowledge

CHITRA #14
(chih' trah)
Virgo 23–20 to Libra 6–40

Translation: Brilliant
Symbol: A pearl
Deity: Twastri (twahsh' tree), the Celestial Architect; or Vishwakarma, the God of Vastu
Marker Star: α Alpha Virginis or Spica (spee' kah; spy' kah)
Dasa Planet: Mars
Key Concept: Attainment of the most beautiful things on the spiritual and material level items

SWATI #15

(swah' tee)

Libra 6–40 to Libra 20–00

Translation: Sword
Symbol: A sword
Deity: Vayu (vah' yoo) the Wind
Marker Star: α Alpha Bootis (boh oh' teez) or Arcturus
Dasa Planet: Rahu
Key Concept: Cutting away ignorance and being what we truly are; self-sufficiency; discovering the source

VISHAKHA #16

(vee shah' kah)

Libra 20–00 to Scorpio 3–20

Translation: Forked branch
Symbol: Archway for weddings
Deity: Indra the Powerful, and Agni the Fire God
Marker Star: α Alpha Librae (lee' bree; ly' bree)
Dasa Planet: Jupiter
Key Concept: Preparing a creative field to harvest the benefits within the proper time

ANURADHA #17
(ah noo rah' dah)
Scorpio 3–20 to Scorpio 16–40

Translation: Success (some say "After-Radha" in that Vishaka was also
  called "Radha")
Symbol: Lotus flower, a row or furrow
Deity: Mitra the Friend, God of Friendliness, associated with the daytime Sun
Marker Star: δ Delta Scorpii (skor' pee eye)
Dasa Planet: Saturn
Key Concept: Building and renewing relationships that increase prosperity; developing
  mutual support that leads to friendliness and continuing success

JYESHTHA #18
(jaysh' tah)
Scorpio 16–40 to 0–00 Sagittarius

Translation: The chief one, the eldest or first born
Symbol: Umbrella or hanging earring
Deity: Indra, Chief of Gods
Marker Star: α Alpha Scorpii or Antares (ahn tair' eez)
Dasa Planet: Mercury
Key Concept: Using their experience to properly utilize their resources to get maximum
  gain while still maintaining energy and enthusiasm

MULA #19
(moo' lah)
Sagittarius 0–00 to Sagittarius 13–20

Translation: The root

Symbol: Roots or a lion's tail (a whisk)

Deity: Nirriti, a Goddess of Destruction—some say the Earth, akin to Bhumi, the Earth Goddess

Marker Star: λ Lambda Scorpii

Dasa Planet: Ketu

Key Concept: Examining the "root" cause of problems; gains success by moving out of or destroying the old ways and making satisfying improvements for a fulfilling future

PURVASHADA #20
(pur vah sha' dah)
Sagittarius 13–20 to Sagittarius 26–40

Translation: The former undefeated or unsubdued

Symbol: An elephant's tusk, a fan, or a bed

Deity: Varuna, "all enveloping sky," Lord of Water; some say Apa, another name for water

Marker Star: δ Delta Sagittarii (saj ih tair' ee eye)

Dasa Planet: Venus

Key Concept: Motivated to be liberated from ineffective and inefficient behaviors by cleaning out non-value-added activities in order to reinvigorate the core of who they are and achieve their full potential

UTTARASHADA #21
(oo tah' rah shah' dah)
Sagittarius 26–40 to Capricorn 10–00

Translation: The latter unsubdued

Symbol: A small cot

Deity: Vishwa-Deva—*Vishwa* means "universal" and *Deva* is a term for the gods, refers to the "33 Universal Gods"

Marker Star: σ Sigma Sagittarii

Dasa Planet: Sun

Key Concept: Dedicated to making the spiritual and material alliances work for everyone's benefit; integrating their own value by supporting the values of others; supporting and supported by following what they know to be right and staying within the natural way of things

SHRAVANA #22
(shrah' vah nah)
Capricorn 10–00 to Capricorn 23–20

Translation: The listener

Symbol: Ear (listening), an arrow, a trident

Deity: Vishnu the All Pervading, one of the Trimurtis—the three operators or gunas of the Universe along with Shiva and Brahma

Marker Star: α Alpha Aquilae (ah' kwil ee) or Altair

Dasa Planet: Moon

Key Concept: Effective listener; gets support and success from building rapport, and interacting effectively with others

DHANISTHA #23
(dah neesh' tah)
Capricorn 23–20 to Aquarius 6–40

Translation: Wealthy
Symbol: A drum
Deity: Vasus, the "abode" or "dweller," the Eight Aides of Vishnu
Marker Star: β Beta Delphini (del fee' nee)
Dasa Planet: Mars
Key Concept: Excellence; capacity; influence and abundance derived from aiding and building on the achievement and resources of others

SATABISHA #24
(sah tah bee' shah)
Aquarius 6–40 to Aquarius 20–00

Translation: The hundred physicians
Symbol: A garland of 100 flowers; a circle
Deity: Varuna, the "all-enveloping sky," Ruler of the Waves or Water Deities
Marker Star: λ Lambda Aquarii (ah kwair' ee eye)
Dasa Planet: Rahu
Key Concept: Creating an environment of wholeness where healing and improvement can take place

PURVABHADRAPADA #25
(pur' vah bah' drah pah' dah)
Aquarius 20–00 to Pisces 3–20

Translation: The burning pair (with Uttara Bhadrapada); or the former beautiful foot (note that a "foot" could also be sunlight in the form of a beam or shaft of light), some authors have replaced the word *bhadra* ("beautiful") in this and the following nakshatra, with *proshtha,* which means "an ox" or "a carp."

Symbol: Front legs of a cot or small bed (when "proshtha" is used, some authors represent this nakshatra as a small four-legged footstool)

Deity: Aja Ekapad (ah' jah ehk' ah pahd), a one-footed goat or a sunbeam (*aja* is a name for the sun, *eka* means "one," and *pad* is "foot")

Marker Star: α Alpha Pegasi (peg' uh see), some say Beta Pegasi

Dasa Planet: Jupiter

Key Concept: Purposeful; one-point minded; achieves success after removing obstacles

UTTARABHADRAPADA #26
(oo' tah rah bah' drah pa' dah)
Pisces 3–20 to Pisces 16–40

Translation: The burning pair (along with Purvabhadrapada) or the latter beautiful foot

Deity: Ahirbudhnya, "bottom snake," or a snake or water serpent of the deep or lower Milky Way

Marker Star: γ Gamma Pegasi

Dasa Planet: Saturn

Key Concept: Gives us the ability to connect with the nourishing and sustaining aspects of our personality and the environment around us, leading to maximum growth and a full harvest of benefits

REVATI #27
(ray' vuh tee)
Pisces 16–40 to Aries 0–00

Translation: The wealthy one
Symbol: A fish or a drum
Deity: Pushan the Prosperer, a form of the sun's light at dawn
Marker Star: ζ Zeta Piscium (pish' ee um)
Dasa Planet: Ketu
Key Concept: Benefits by nourishing and sustaining others; challenges are reduced and prosperity increases in service to others

⁕ ⁕ ⁕ ⁕ ⁕ ⁕

Ketu, the South Node of the Moon.

INTRODUCTION TO A TRADITIONAL VEDIC CHART CALCULATION

*Twelve are the fellies (rim sections), and the wheel is single; three are the naves
(axle holes). What man hath understood? Therein are set together spokes three
hundred and sixty, which in nowise can be loosened.*
— Rig Veda, Book 1, 48

While many of the classic Vedic astrology texts instruct you about the various planetary positions that reveal behavior over time, they often don't provide much of an approach to interpreting the chart.

Astrologers have developed their own processes over time, and some of these are held as family secrets and passed down privately through the generations. As you develop in your own practice, you'll discover that there are a wide variety of approaches to chart interpretation. We'll take a quick look at a few high-level processes to chart interpretation that I think will get you going and give you good results.

KARAKA BY KARAKA

There are many ways to examine a chart, but I think the following method will help you the most. This approach is called analyzing astrological indications by the subject matter area—in other words, karaka by karaka. You will find that clients want you to examine the strong or weak and favorable or unfavorable indications of the planetary and bhava karakas (house indications) for specific areas of their lives, such as wealth, health, emotions, relationships, career, education, spirituality, travel, location, and so on. You might find that in the time you have with a client, you'll focus on a set of specific questions as put forth by that person. This is a common practice.

Again, you, as the astrologer, will look for repeating patterns and determine if those patterns are strong or weak and favorable or unfavorable. It's like collecting coins to see what the value of each is and how many you have. They all add up, by quality and quantity, to a specific total value. This might seem a bit daunting at first, but go through it word by word, planet by planet, and it will become second nature after some experience.

Each of these life areas, or karakas, have specific planetary indicators that will give you insight into what a person's karma or potential outcomes might be. By examining the karaka or signifying planets, signs, houses, and the planets aspecting, ruling, or combining in terms of these indicators, you'll get a good idea about the potential of that area of life.

You can perform your analysis from the Lagna, Sun, and Moon. You can add in the navamsa Lagna, if you want to go a bit further. (As a beginner, it's okay just to start out looking from the Lagna. You can add the others later.) Count each of these as the first house, and analyze the planets, signs, and houses from each of them. Look for repeating patterns and score the planets by their strength and favorableness—that is to say, how much and how good the astrological indicators are.

At this beginner's level, you can give more weight to the Lagna (50 percent), then the Moon (25 percent), then the Sun (15 percent). You can also perform a similar analysis on the navamsa chart giving it about 10 percent importance as well. Again you can evaluate the planets like coins and currency. They will each have their own value in a chart, according to how their influence is improved or degraded by mixing in with other planets. It might be that one planetary coin will be naturally worth a quarter and another might be worth a dollar. Then in the interaction of the chart, the quarter planet gets revalued to a dollar, and the dollar planet gets knocked down a bit because of aspects to it and its location. One indicator might have only quarters associated with it, but it has ten quarters, while another indicator might have a dollar's worth of value, but then there's only one. We see this very principle in coin collecting: Someone might have a quarter that's worth ten dollars and a dollar that is worth only five dollars. So look at the quality and the quantity of planetary indicators and add them all up. Again, this is a skill of synthesis that will develop over time with experience.

The Vedic astrologer analyzes the birth chart to find the correspondences between the macrocycles of nature and the individual microcycles of the client.

237

VULNERABILITY ASSESSMENT:
Finding the Overall Strength of the Chart

Remember that the chart needs to be strong overall and have good *bala,* or "strength," to manifest meaningful success in any of the areas under examination. The key to a bala score can be seen in the favorableness and strength related to the Lagna and its ruler. You can also apply these rules to the Moon, Sun, and navamsa Lagna to get a comprehensive picture of the chart's strength or lack of it.

As mentioned, you can give a greater weight to the influence of the Lagna, then count from the Moon, then the Sun, and finally from the navamsa Lagna. I think these will get you pretty close. The following pointers offer some examples of what is weak and unfavorable in the chart, judging from the Lagna. Note that some astrologers tend to focus on weakness, their thinking being that if something is good, it won't be any problem, so they just look for what's "broken." Unfortunately, this can lead some clients and observers to think that astrology is a negative practice, which of course it isn't—it's the Science of Light!

- The Lagna is occupied or aspected by malefics.

- The Lagna ruler is poorly placed (especially if located in dusthanas 6, 8, and 12).

- The Lagna ruler is conjunct or aspected by malefics (especially dusthana rulers).

- There are a number (three or more) of weakened or negative planets (sandhi, debilitated, conjunct or aspected by malefics, combust the Sun, weak and retrograde, etc.) in the chart.

You can review the material in this book on strength and weakness of planets to understand the strength and favorableness factors more. Of course, the reverse of the above would indicate good bala and the ability to prosper in life. But most people come for a reading because something isn't working right in their lives, so knowing how to identify areas of vulnerability will help you help your clients to help themselves. Just make sure you also speak to the client's strengths to help fortify them and remind them of their capacity to improve their lives. Clients will come to you for both direction and comfort . . . and it might be that they don't necessarily want to follow the direction, they just want to have it.

If you find several of these negative indicators in a chart analysis, then the chart will have less strength to counteract negative events. The person might lack the initial power to promote themselves properly to thrive in certain areas of life. Nothing is hopeless, it's just that some things take more work, and that might be that person's mission in this life—to get better in these areas. Remedial measures help in this regard.

Here are some of the ways to judge a few key karaka areas that many people ask about:

Career (Karaka Planet: Sun; Karaka House: Tenth): First, look at the Sun; the ruler of the house the Sun is placed in (called the dispositor of the Sun); location of the Sun's dispositor in terms of signs and houses and what is located and/or aspecting the Sun's dispositor; location of the Sun itself by sign, house, and conjunctions or aspects falling on it.

Next, look toward the tenth house and sign; ruler of the tenth; location of the ruler of the tenth planets conjunct and/or aspecting the ruler of the tenth.

Then you can take the ruler of the tenth in the natal chart and see where it's located in the navamsa chart. Look then at what planet is ruling that rasi planet in the navamsa. (This sounds a bit complicated, but work through it slowly and you'll see the process falls into place.) This will give further indications for career based on the characteristics of that planet and how strong it is. This formula is called *"ruler of the navamsa of ruler of the tenth."* It's another one of those mind bogglers, but again, think it through and you'll get it. Don't forget that you can also look to the Lagna, its ruler, and planets occupying and aspecting the Lagna to get some clues about career as well. The career indications will be seen from the planets involved with the Lagna. The same can be done from the Moon.

Relationships (Karaka Planet: Venus, but also look at Jupiter for the male in a female's chart; Karaka House: Seventh for marriage, and fifth house for romance): The first step is to evaluate Venus; the ruler of the house Venus is placed in (the dispositor of the Venus); location of Venus's dispositor in terms of signs and houses and what is located and/or aspecting Venus's dispositor; location of Venus itself by sign, house, and conjunctions or aspects falling on it.

Then study the seventh house and sign; ruler of the seventh; location of the ruler of the seventh, planets conjunct and/or aspecting the ruler of the seventh. You would follow the same pattern for the fifth house, the house of romantic love.

Finally, you can look at the favorableness of the navamsa Lagna, the seventh navamsa, and where the ruler of the seventh in the rasi or birth chart is located in the navamsa, and what its ruler is.

These indicators will tell you if you and/or your partner are good candidates for marriage or a committed relationship. You can also use these indicators to see how anyone might fare in terms of working with others.

You might wonder why it seems that a person doesn't have good relationship karma, yet a specific person is still attracted to them . . . maybe this is you! You will find that there's a good deal of attraction generated between two charts when there are conjunctions and/or oppositions of the Lagna, Lagna ruler, Moon, and Sun between the two charts. Passion in the relationship is generally seen when one person's Venus or Mars is conjunct or opposite where Venus and Mars are in the others person's chart—especially by sign. But just because you're attracted to a person doesn't mean you should pick them for a life partner. Understanding this will keep you from feeling too torn or conflicted when you like or love a person, but can't seem to get along with them over time and space.

KEYWORD MATCHING

Another way to interpret a chart, and a good approach for beginners and experts alike, is to use keyword matching. As you've no doubt noticed in reading this book so far, a keyword, or a few summary words, have been identified for each planet, sign, and house. By combining these words in specific patterns you can generate a decent summary interpretation of a chart.

Planet: Each planet in a chart indicates specific traits of behavior. Sage Parashara says that the planets, or grahas, deliver our karma. They indicate aspects of the nature of the person whose chart you're interpreting. Each planet can be identified by a keyword. For example, the Moon indicates feelings, or how "I feel." Mercury indicates how "I think." Venus shows us how "I relate," and so on. These traits are listed under each planet in Chapter 3 of this book.

Sign: Generally, the signs can be used to identify the strength of planets according to where that planet is located, by degree, within that sign. The signs also add further identity to the planet. They reveal the nature or characteristics of the sign, positive or negative, as indicated by the traits of ruler of the sign. For example, Libra is the sign of business, partnerships, and balance. A planet placed in that sign will be modified to reflect a merger with those business or relationship characteristics. The Moon signifies our feelings, so it could represent, in Libra, a feeling for business or a nurturing disposition in relationships. The Moon also indicates traits of teaching or counseling. So with Moon in Libra we could use the keywords to say "counseling or teaching business."

House: The houses in the chart contain the planets and the signs. They bring the influences of the heavens down to earth and show the various states of being or moods of life. The planet will act in favorable or unfavorable ways according to the house it's located in. For example, if a planet is located in the second house, it will exercise its abilities and inclinations within the field of accumulating money, food, speech, and so on. So following our example, the Moon in Libra in the second house could be "counseling," "business," or "speech." Perhaps the person made money as a professional counselor or speaker. The degree to which this person would excel in these traits would be seen in the strength of the planets in the signs, and how favorable they are by the nature of the house they occupy, and what aspects and occupations come upon it.

Making Associations: Keep trying different combinations with people you know. Start the planet sentences with "I" or "my." For example: Saturn is fear or feeling inadequate, so you can say, "I fear . . ." or "I feel inadequate," then add in the keywords taken from indications or karakas of the house and sign where the planet is located. Obviously, if you're doing this for another person, you could change the "I" statements to "you" or "they."

Here's an example of how to interpret the Moon in Libra in the second house:

Moon Keyword Statement: I have a feeling or need for . . . .

Moon in Sign Keyword Statement: [Moon] I have a feeling for [Libra] business and partnerships.

Moon in House Keyword Statement: [Moon] I have a feeling for [second house] accumulating money, or I accumulate money through Moon indications [education, counseling, etc.].

Now combine the three factors. You can be creative at this point and do a three-part word association. Experiment with various combinations and practice with charts of people you know until you get a feel for this technique.

In the example above, you could put together feeling, accumulating, and business. You could say, "Feelings [Moon] for accumulating [second house] via creating balance or business [Libra]."

You can also use keyword matching to indicate the following:

- The effect of a planet in another planet's house or sign, such as Mercury in Saturn's sign. Mercury is in Capricorn, so you get the effect of a Mercury/Saturn combination.

- Planets conjunct or aspecting each other, for example Moon and Venus are located together in Scorpio, so it's like a Moon/Venus combination. The Moon and Venus are in Mars's sign (Scorpio), so we get Moon/Mars and Venus/Mars influence as well.

- One planet transiting over another planet in the birth chart. Assume that Saturn by transit is positioned over Jupiter in Aries, for a specific time of analysis. So there's a Saturn/Jupiter combination, a Jupiter/Mars (Jupiter is in Mars's sign of Aries), and the same with Saturn/Mars.

Knowing what the planets indicate and how they work in combination with other planets is a key to good chart analysis. You also look at how strong and favorable the participating planets are (or aren't) and draw further reference from that.

STEPS FOR INTERPRETING A CHART

We make our fortunes and call it fate.
— Benjamin Disraeli

Again, start out by doing the charts of people you know. Ask them questions to help you clarify your own understanding. Then do the charts of public figures and look at their biographies. Little by little, your knowledge and confidence will build. It's difficult to be right when you're too concerned about being wrong.

As with learning anything, it helps to have a system or process to follow. The following pointers are a blend of Vedic principles coupled with my own many years of experience in chart interpretation. I think these steps, while at a somewhat high level, will get you on your way.

Step 1: Consider the overall chart. Again, get an overview of the chart's general favorable or unfavorable and strong or weak nature. Now you know of the concept of bala, so you'll want to examine the chart for its inherent strength or the lack of it. If the chart has a number of unfavorable and weak characteristics, the more positive indications of the personality will have difficulty expressing themselves and the person will have less capacity to defend themselves against negativity, whatever is the case.

For example, if a field is dry and unwatered and a match falls on it, it will burst into flame. The field is *vulnerable* to fire. The same field, if watered, green and well-tended, can have that same match drop on it, but it won't turn into a raging inferno. Perhaps it will smoke a bit, but the fire will have trouble catching on. If there's an attendant nearby, they will also help put the fire out or call for help. The green field has bala, the brown field doesn't. Same event, different responses according to strength.

When determining the strength of planets, the key is this: In general, planets will be strong or weak according to their placement in a sign. *Strong* means the planet exhibits its indications or characteristics and is capable of repelling any negative effects coming on to it from other parts of the chart. *Weak* means the planet can't fully express its indications and has trouble when encountering negative influences from other parts of the chart.

Strong planetary placements are shown by the following:

- In sign of exaltation, moolatrikona, or own sign

- Yoga karaka or prosperity planet as see by specific rising signs

- Location between benefic planets *(shuba kartari)*

- Conjunct or aspected by benefic planets

- Strong planets participating in favorable yogas also lifts the chart quite a bit

- In the middle of a sign *(bhava madya)*

- Being in the same sign in the rasi and the navamsa *(vargottama)*

- High (over one point) Shadbala scores (1.0 or greater, as calculated by a software program)

Weak planetary placements are indicated by these factors:

- In sign of debilitation

- Location between malefic planets *(papa kartari)*

- Conjunct or aspected by malefic planets

- Weak planets participating in favorable yogas don't lift the chart quite as much

- Sandhi or placed at the very beginning under one degree in a sign, or at the very end over 29 degrees

- Low (under one point) Shadbala scores (such as .99 or less, as calculated by a software program)

Classical texts in Vedic astrology offer a very detailed system for calculating planetary strength. This system uses six specific planetary conditions to determine strength and is therefore called *Shadbala*, or "six strengths." Luckily, today Shadbala is becoming more popular because of the fast calculations of astrology software. You will see the word *Shadbala* on most Vedic astrology chart printouts, and you'll also see a number assigned as a ratio or percentage. Any planet with a score above one is deemed to be strong and is considered weak if under one point. It's still advisable to follow additional methods of determining strength to ensure you get the right evaluation overall. Just be careful not to count Shadbala calculations twice.

Remember that in general, planets will be favorable or unfavorable according to their placement in a house. *Favorable* means the planet is advantageous and helpful in manifesting the positive features and successful outcomes anticipated in the chart. Some astrologers use the word "auspicious" in that the planet indicates the possibility of good fortune or positive results. *Unfavorable* means the planet isn't advantageous, and obstructs rather than helps in manifesting positive features. It forms a barrier and isn't conducive to the successful outcomes anticipated in the chart. "Inauspicious" is also used in this regard.

Favorable planetary placements are shown by:

- Location in trines (houses 1, 5, and 9)

- Location in angles (houses 1, 4, 7, and 10)

- Location in the second and eleventh houses are considered good. These are generally regarded as money houses. The third house is somewhat unfavorable, but can deliver good outcomes since it indicates courage, determination, and creative self-expression.

Unfavorable planetary placements are shown by:

- Location in dusthanas (houses 6, 8, and 12). (Note that the sixth house is an *upachaya,* or "growing" house, and can get better over time. Additional upachaya houses that indicate favorableness over time are the third, tenth, and eleventh houses.)

Step 2: Look at the *quantity* of the strong/weak or favorable/unfavorable planetary placements in the chart. Add up the positive and negative factors for each planet to determine if it will express its favorable or unfavorable characteristics. Sometimes there will be a mix of both, so you might see average results or unsteady development where the person has periods of time when things are okay and times when they're really not. Likewise, they may be good in certain conditions or settings and bad in others.

Step 3: Study the following chart features for each karaka or significant life area. Examine these bulleted indicators for areas such as health, wealth, relationships, career, and so forth. See how these areas of life are influenced in terms of strong/weak and favorable/unfavorable planetary indicators associated with them. After a bit of analysis, you'll most likely see a trend emerging. Mark down these repeating patterns—this is what will tend to happen

For further karakas or significations, examine the following from the Lagna, Moon, and the Sun:

- The rising sign or the first house (as well as counting the Moon and then the Sun as the first house)

- The location of the rising sign ruler by sign and house and conjunctions or aspects falling on it

- Planets aspecting and located in the rising sign

- The sign occupying the karaka houses and areas of life under consideration

- The location of the karaka house ruler by sign and house and conjunctions or aspects falling on it

- Planets aspecting and located in the karaka house

- Location of the karaka by sign and house

- Planets conjunct or aspecting the karaka planet

Now, go to Step 4 to start compiling your findings.

Step 4: Start synthesizing and tallying repeating patterns of planetary characteristics. Jot down your observations. This will help you record what you uncover and aid in summarizing your findings.

If you start to see a planetary trait repeating three or more times, you're most likely seeing a pattern that will express itself in that person's life. Remember to evaluate its strength/weakness and favorable/unfavorable character to see the quality and quantity of its influence, in addition to the amount of times it occurs in the chart. For example, if you see Mars's influence by sign, house, and aspect repeating in several places, as judged from the Lagna, Sun, and Moon, you can begin to suspect that the person will demonstrate Mars-type attitudes and traits.

Up to this point, you've learned the basics of interpreting a chart, be it for a person or an event. This level of analysis is considered more static in that you're dealing with past events. The chart actually represents the karma that you brought into this lifetime. It's like driving while looking through the rearview mirror. In the next chapter, we'll explore the more predictive side of Vedic astrology, which uses the chart to forecast events. This is the more dynamic side of Vedic astrology analysis. It enables you to anticipate the approach of a dangerous event so you can fortify yourself against it, or it can help predict positive events to maximize them in the future. It's more like driving with a good map, looking ahead through the front window, with the headlights on, after a great night's sleep, with a nice snack to munch along the way, and a full tank of gas!

Ganesh is the patron deity of Vedic astrologers. He represents the energy that helps remove any obstructions that might interfere with a proper Vedic astrology chart analysis.

Chapter Nine

Keys to Vedic
Chart Forecasting

*One who reads or listens with attention and devotion to
this most excellent Hora Shastra becomes long lived and is
blessed with increase in strength, wealth, and good reputation.*
— Brihat Parashara Hora Shastra, Chapter 97

Now that you've finished this *static* phase of chart analysis, the next step will be to shift to the *dynamic* side of Vedic astrology, and that is chart forecasting. Once a planet's characteristics are identified according to its placement in a sign and house, we learn that the resulting behavior identified with that planet will change or express itself differently over time. This is what is unique about astrology as an assessment tool: It not only discusses the nature or behavior of individuals, but projects how that behavior might unfold over time.

How events might express themselves in time is shown to a large degree by the *dasa* (dah' shah), or "planetary period," operating during the time period under consideration. This is taken along with the conditioning influence of *gochara* (go char' ah), or "transits"—that is, the orbiting planets in motion at the time over the fixed natal positions. Dasa and gochara tell which planet is acting at a certain time and notify you what results to expect from them over time, as promised in the natal chart. You won't get a result that doesn't exist to some degree in the natal chart.

As a new student of Vedic astrology, you don't need to go to this phase right away. This is a more advanced skill than chart synthesis, and an area where many newer astrologers are hesitant to tread. But you can at least learn some of the rules of the road for forecasting and go down that avenue later when you're ready. My first book, *Beneath a Vedic Sky,* covers dasa and gochara and other forecasting techniques in more detail.

Basic Principles of the Dasa System

Planetary dasa rulers "turn on" a planet's indications as seen in the birth chart. The dasa ruling planets each have an allotted time span of influence. This is calculated by a formula that takes the position of your Moon at birth, uses nakshatra tables, and determines which planet's influence will be in effect for a designated period of time. The sum total of all the periods amounts to a 120-year cycle. Perhaps if we take good care of ourselves we could live that long! The enclosed software or other Vedic programs can determine this for you automatically, so there's no need to get into the detail of calculation here.

Again, be mindful that these techniques can't produce results that aren't promised in the natal chart. A timing period for kingly results will bring improvement during the proper cycle, but if the person has a lot of nonkingly attributes, the results will be better, but perhaps not necessarily kingly. The results will be favorable or unfavorable depending

Planetary period	Length of Time
Ketu	7 years
Venus	20 years
Sun	6 years
Moon	10 years
Mars	7 years
Rahu	18 years
Jupiter	16 years
Saturn	19 years
Mercury	17 years

Planetary periods: Each planet has an allotted period of time to express itself for the positive or negative during the term of a person's life. Knowing the nature and time of the planetary period can help us work to our strengths and fortify our weaknesses.

upon the condition of the planet in the natal chart (as well as other factors).

As I've said, a planet that's well placed by sign and house can be expected to give more positive results. The indica-

tions forecast by the dasa ruling planet will be further modified by the influence of gochara, or planetary transits. There are also sub-dasa periods, called *bhuktis* (bhook' tees), and sub-sub-dasa periods called *antaradasa* (ahn' tah rah dah' shah). You'll see these on computer print-outs. These three periods all need to all be taken into account and merged together to get an "average" of what's going on or might go on. Again, this takes time and skill to develop and isn't a central focus of this beginner's book. Just keep in mind, as you did with the static birth chart, that you have to merge the various forecasting techniques into a consistent whole for the chart and time period being examined.

Be aware that dasa periods are very sensitive to accurate birth times. The timing of the start and ending of dasa periods will vary from days to even months from differences in the birth time. A correct time of birth is a must for a good interpretation.

GOCHARA, THE TRANSIT OF PLANETS

The transit or movement of the planets at the current time, a time you're examining in the past, or a time you're projecting forward, will influence the static condition of the birth chart. Judge the favorable or unfavorable effects of transiting planets using the same rules that you use to evaluate planets in the birth chart. You'll find that the closer to exact degree the transiting planet is to the natal planet, the more significant the effect. Look at the calendar to see on what days these lineups occur and look for the favorable, mixed, or unfavorable results from there. This is a very simple rule, but it's very effective in determining when the results forecast by the transit will most likely show up.

Favorable transits: If a planet is favorable by transit and transits over a favorable place (sign or house) in the birth chart, the event will be positive.

Average or mixed transits: If a planet is favorable by transit and moves over an unfavorable place in the birth chart, then the results will be mixed or average. You could equate it to calculating grade-point averages like you do in school. If a transiting planet is an A grade, but is transiting over a C-grade location, then the A planet will be good for the C location, but the C location will not be so good for the A planet. The result will be a more mediocre performance, maybe a B, where the A doesn't get to shine, but then the C becomes a little bit better.

You can reverse this with the same effect—that is, judging the results of an unfavorable planet over a favorable position in the birth chart. The unfavorable transiting planet gets a boost by traveling over some good territory in the chart.

Unfavorable transits: If a planet is unfavorable by transit and transits over an unfavorable place (sign or house) in the birth chart, the event will most likely be

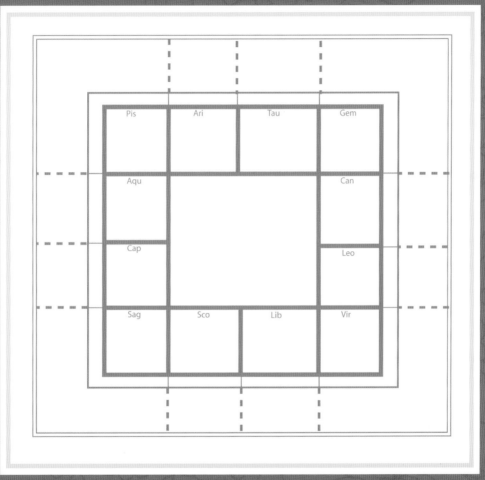

Pis	Ari	Tau	Gem
Aqu			Can
Cap			Leo
Sag	Sco	Lib	Vir

Natal and transit form: You can use a form like this to place the transiting planets around border of the signs and houses of the natal chart to see what planets are influencing the various signs and houses by transit. You can also mark the planet that's ruling the dasa period to detect the influences happening during the planetary period, as reflected in the natal chart.

negative or unfavorable. If a D-grade planet passes over a D-grade location, it can't help it much at all, and the below average state from the transiting planet and the birth planet stay in place.

Merge transit effects with the quality of the dasa period: You do have to merge in the dasa effects and take the grade-point average concept a bit further. If the transiting planet and the place transited over in the chart are unfavorable, but the dasa period is very favorable, then the result of the transit won't be so unfavorable . . . it gets lifted up by the quality of the period overall. The reverse will also be true in that the influence of a favorable transit will be diminished by occurring during an unfavorable dasa period.

Ganesh is considered the remover of obstacles and is prayed to at the beginning of important events in the hopes of removing any obstructions, setbacks, or delays.

CHAPTER TEN

REMEDIAL MEASURES: TUNING AND CORRECTING THE WAVES OF LIFE

The planet who is the cause of adverse effects to a person at any time should be worshipped and appeased because Brahma has blessed the planets with the boon, "Do good to the person who worships you."
— Brihat Parashara Hora Shastra, Chapter 84, Slokas 26–27

Vedic astrology informs us of the root cause of our behaviors and what good or bad inclinations we brought into this life. Being a preventive system, Vedic astrology also tells us what things we need to avoid or to do in order to avert danger. There are problems from doing what's wrong, and problems from not doing what's right. Remedial measures are provided as a means to correct our action so that we stay in alignment with the forces of nature (the devas and their planetary influences), and that we get maximum benefit in life.

When we put our attention on positive traits and outcomes, as represented by the characteristics held by each planet and their associated deity or life force, those characteristics and intentions get stronger in our life. If we focus on, praise, and venerate positive qualities in any form, from a relaxed and respectful state of mind, we're blessed. By placing our attention on them, those traits get amplified within ourselves. At a minimum we pay back on our negative karmic debt, thus our cosmic "credit score" goes up and we can purchase more joy in life.

Deities are often represented in symbolic, concrete forms, such as paintings and statues, to help us focus on the feelings they represent. In their simplest form, the devas are expressions of impulses of nature. They're seen outside us in the display and

Vedic priests performing a remedial measure called a "yagya."

core rhythms of nature, and within us in our various emotions. For example, Mitra is the Lord of Friendliness, but in essence is the "feeling" of friendliness as well. When we own the feeling of friendliness, then all creatures become friends with us. We're essentially "them" in that respect. We get united through that common feeling . . . we *are* that common feeling.

Some typical remedial measures or counterbalances to negativity and weakness include the following:

- *Yagyas,* or Vedic rituals to place a person in tune with natural law

- *Ratnas,* or gemstones aimed at either calming or empowering planets in the chart

- *Mantras,* or coherence-generating sounds used in silent meditation

- *Japa,* or the recitation of mantras as counted aloud on *malas* (rosary-like prayer beads)

- *Yantras,* or visual meditation aids

- *Vratas,* or vows (like New Year's resolutions)

- *Dana,* or charity. (Charity can be time or money, or whatever resources we have to fill a need somewhere. It's common in India to give gifts to Brahmans, or priests, in this regard.)

Additional Vedic remedial and preventative approaches are Vastu, for living in correct structures; and Ayurveda, with its *panchakarma,* or "five actions," for cleansing the body and preventing disease. It's important to get your remedial recommendations through an established Vedic astrologer, Ayurvedic physician, or Vastu expert. Direct contact with an experienced practitioner will be the safer way to go.

TRADITIONAL CRITERIA FOR WEARING ASTROLOGICAL GEMSTONES

Planet	Color	Gem	Gem Finger	Metal	Weekday
Sun	Dark red, orange	Ruby	Ring	Copper	Sunday
Moon	Bright white	Pearl	Little	Silver	Monday
Mars	Middle red	Red coral	Ring	Gold	Tuesday
Mercury	Grass green	Emerald	Little	Silver	Wednesday
Jupiter	Golden, yellow	Yellow sapphire	Index	Gold	Thursday
Venus	Middle white	Diamond	Little	Silver	Friday

Planet	Color	Gem	Gem Finger	Metal	Weekday
Saturn	Black, blue	Blue sapphire	Middle	Iron	Saturday
Rahu	Brownish	Hessonite garnet	Middle	Panchadhatu (5 metals)	Saturday (like Saturn)
Ketu	Stripes, multicolor, blue-green	Cat's-eye (chrysoberyl)	Ring*	Panchadhatu (5 metals)	Tuesday (like Mars)

Note: Astrologers vary as to which finger to wear a ring on. For example, some authors state that a cat's-eye for Ketu can be worn on the little finger.

A navaratna, or nine-stone pendant used to obtain blessings from the nine planets (this configuration is also worn in finger rings and bracelets).

267

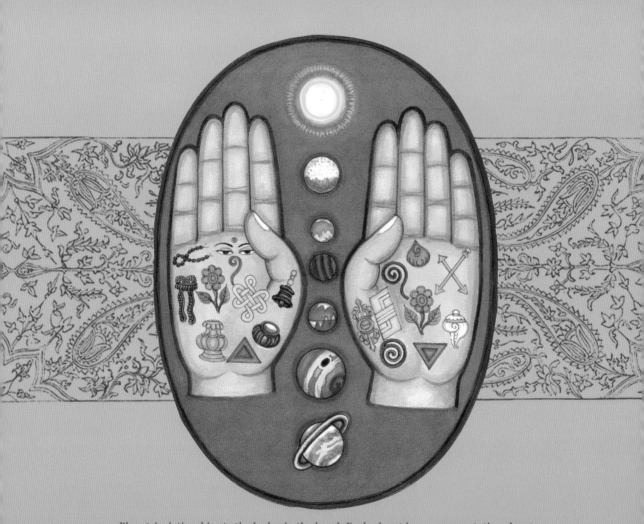

Planets' relationships to the body via the hand: Each planet has a representative planet associated with a particular gemstone and a particular finger, and wearing the proper gemstone helps balance the influences associated with planets.

Planet	Deity *(According to Parasara)*	Popular Modern Deity	Person Represented
Sun	Agni (fire)	Vishnu or Surya	Father
Moon	Varuna (water)	Parvati	Mother
Mars	Subramanya (Shiva's son)	Subramaniya or Shiva	Siblings
Mercury	Mahavishnu (Maintainer)	Saraswati	Cousin
Jupiter	Indra (Lord of Devas)	Brihaspati or Dakshina Murti	Children
Venus	Indrani or Sachi Devi (Wife of Indra)	Lakshmi	Partner
Saturn	Brahma	Shiva or Durga	Old Persons
Rahu	None Given	Durga or Sarpa (Cobra)	Grandmother
Ketu	None Given	Ganesh	Grandfather

Vishnu, the All Pervasive One, representing the Sun: A very popular deity amongst followers of the Vaishnava tradition in India, he represents that aspect of nature that maintains the universe. Vishnu is part of the Hindu trinity called the Trimurti (three bodies), along with his counterparts Brahma and Shiva. This triumvirate also represents the three gunas, those qualities or prime operating principles of nature.

Parvati (par' vah tee), the Mountain Dweller, representing the Moon: Parvati is shown as the shakti, or "power," of the strong matriarch of the family. She epitomizes the loving energy of Shiva's wife fulfilling her destiny as the mother of two of India's equally powerful deities, Ganesh (gah nesh') and Subramaniya (soo' brah mahn' ee yah). As such, she carries the energy of the nurturing Moon. As we will see, the nature of feminine shakti is presented in different forms in Vedic literature. We have Shiva's spouse represented under various names and energies, such as Uma (oo' mah) the Favorable, Gauri (gow' ree) the Fair One, Kali (kah' lee) the Dark-Skinned, and Chandi (chahn' dee) the Fierce or Impetuous.

Saraswati (sah' rahs swah' tee), the Flowing One, representing Mercury: In Sanskrit, sara means "essence" and swa means "self." Some also interpret this as "flowing one," associating her with the famous river that bears her name. This flow also represents a stream of stars in the Milky Way and is said to be a specific nerve or energy flow in the body. Saraswati is the power that represents knowledge, learning, and musical expression—all traits associated with the planet Mercury.

Subramaniya, the Pious One, representing Mars: Shiva and his wife Parvati had two famous offspring—Ganesh and Subramaniya. As a young child of Shiva, Subramaniya represents the innocent, vigorous energy associated with the planet Mars. It's the custom in India to try to pacify the otherwise fierce and intense-acting Mars with a soft, pleasing name.

Lakshmi Yantra. A representation of the qualities and power of the Vedic goddess shown in a geometric form.

Lakshmi (lahk' shmee), *the Purposeful One, representing Venus: Lakshmi actually comes from the Sanskrit word* laksya, *which means "target" or "purpose." She represents the power to gain our objectives of wealth and prosperity, in terms of both the material and spiritual worlds. She represents all that is feminine and refined, which are key indications of the planet Venus. Lakshmi is also a favorite among women in India.*

Shiva, the Auspicious One, representing Saturn: Shiva is one of the trimurtis, along with Vishnu and Brahma. He represents the power of quiescence, and as such is sometimes called the Lord of Silence. Thus he is looked upon by his followers, the "Shaivites," as much a creative force as a destructive one. Shiva is linked to Kala, the ruler of time, and thus has an association with Saturn, who is the lord of control and ultimately of death—the cessation of time.

Durga, the Fortified One, representing Rahu: Durga represents the power of nature that preserves moral order and makes one "invincible" in taking correct action in the world. Durga is a form of the Divine Mother who expresses her indomitable power to guard the world from harmful influences. She is called upon to destroy the energy of negative forces, such as misplaced self-interest, resentment, intolerance, extremism, antagonism, and egoism. The clarity and power she brings parallels Rahu's power to bring material blessings and remove the shadows that darken one's life.

Brihaspati, the Lord of Prayers or the Lord of the Voice, also the Guru representing Jupiter: Brihaspati is the guru of the devas, or the positive forces of nature. His father is Angiras, one of the rishis generated by Brahma, the Creator. Brihaspati, in his role of guru, gave much advice to the devas in their battles against the asuras. The role of counselor links Brihaspati to the wisdom aspect of Jupiter.

Ganesh, the Lord of the Ganas, representing Ketu: Ganesh, the son of Shiva, is described as having control over the legion of beings called "ganas" who are special attendants of Shiva. Ganesh is a much-loved deity in India and is associated with his name, Ganapati, and his special shakti to be able to remove obstacles, setbacks, and delays. Ganesh's elephant symbolism gives him great strength, coupled with his human body, which amplifies his intelligence. The mouse that accompanies Ganesh shows his capacity to reach into the smallest regions in every nook and cranny of existence.

Krishna (krish' nah) the Black, is represented as an incarnation of Vishnu, the Preserver. Krishna is shown in many forms, such as in the guise of Dhanvantari, the Lord of Ayurveda.

Dhanvantari, the Lord of Ayurveda.

CHAPTER ELEVEN

SUPPLEMENTAL VEDIC SYSTEMS: AYURVEDA AND VASTU

Vedic systems of knowledge enliven the inner intelligence of the body and thereby maintain the vitality of the physiology, and also maintains a healthy relationship between the body and its counterparts in the physiology of the Cosmic Body— the Sun, Moon, planets, and stars—through Jyotish, Ayurveda, Vastu Shastra, and all other aspects of the Vedic Literature.
— Maharishi Mahesh Yogi

AYURVEDA: THE SCIENCE OF HEALTH

Ayurveda is a preventive health system developed in ancient India. It performs its analysis of well-being based on three body types, called *vata, pitta,* and *kapha.* As I mentioned previously, Vedic knowledge is an integrated system. All of its components fit logically and completely into a whole systems structure. Ayurveda, as well as Vedic astrology and Vastu, focuses on balancing the elements—air, earth, fire, and water. If there's an excess or a deficiency of any of these elements, then illness arises. Knowing how the planets express themselves in terms of the three Ayurvedic body types will give you additional clues when interpreting a chart.

In classical Ayurveda, the *vaidya*, or Ayurvedic practitioner ("doctor"), diagnoses the patient through their pulse and sometimes their tongue. The patient's natal chart is also examined, along with the current planetary transits (gochara), plan-

etary periods (dasa), and the chart for the moment of arrival at the office (prasna). The astrological diagrams for birth time and the moment of office arrival, coupled with the pulse diagnosis, give the doctor a comprehensive tool set for diagnosis. This tells the doctor the core constitution of the individual along with temporary modifications caused by the planetary effects of dasa and gochara.

How Does Ayurveda Work?

Astrologically, the planets reign over bhutas, the elements or basic building

The Ayurvedic doctor examines the patient via pulse diagnosis, as well as through the analysis of a Vedic astrology chart.

blocks of creation. Sun and Mars represent Agni, fire; Moon and Venus reign over Apa or Jal, water and fluids; Mercury rules Prithivi or earth; Saturn is the Lord of Vayu, air; and Jupiter is regent of Akasha, or space.

Ayurveda condenses the five elements into the three major groups: vata, pitta, and kapha. Ayurveda's basic view is that all of life—people, food, creatures, environment, and diseases—are combinations of the three elementals of air (vata), fire (pitta), and earth—with some water—which is called kapha. When these three constitutional elements are balanced, one is healthy. Illness is defined as an imbalance or excess of these elements. All health problems can be traced to defects of one or more elements, or *doshas*.

Vata

Vata is a quality of life that's related to the air element. It governs all the activities in the body. Everything moves, or blows, on the currents of vata. Vata qualities are: light (as air), dry, cold, and variable. People who have a predominance of vata, as indicated by the dominant planets in their chart, are generally thin and quick-moving. They learn and forget quickly, and are subject to quick changes in feeling. Vata, when out of balance, expresses itself in poor digestion with gas, dry skin, cold limbs, cracking joints, fitful sleeping, emotional swings, exhaustion, overactivity, worry, and nervousness. Many imbalances have vata at their root. Vata people are like birds flying around.

*Life flows in the manifestation of the three gunas (qualities),
to the five bhutas (elements), out to the nine grahas (planets).*

Elementals: Air or wind (with some akasha, or space)

Planets and Signs: Mercury, Saturn, weak Moon, and Venus; also, Rahu can act like Saturn. In addition, the signs ruled by these planets: Gemini, Virgo, Capricorn, Aquarius, a weak Cancer, Libra, and Taurus.

Pitta

Pitta is a life force that is related to the energy of fire. Pitta consumes. It's related to strong digestion and hunger, heat or redness in the body, clear speech and thought, motivation, and warmth of expression. Anger, frustration, exasperation, impatience, and extreme hunger are signs that pitta is out of balance in your body. Pitta people have a medium body build—not too muscular, not too thin. Pitta expresses itself in ailments such as indigestion, ulcers, rashes, fevers, cuts, wounds, bruises, redness, and other inflammatory conditions. Pittas are like tigers.

Elementals: Fire or heat

Planets and Signs: Sun and Mars, also Ketu can act like Mars. In addition, the signs ruled by these planets: Aries, Leo, and Scorpio.

Kapha

Kapha is a bodily constitution that's derived from the combination of earth and a little bit of the water element. Kapha is mostly viewed as earthy, so it governs the strength and structure of the body in general. Being watery, it shows itself in imbalances such as fluid buildup, fat, colds, coughs, congestion, general stagnation, and lethargy. Kapha people are either calm and balanced or lazy and indulgent. Kaphas are strongly built and have endurance. Kaphas are like elephants.

Elementals: Earth (and some water)
Planets and Signs: Moon, Jupiter, and Venus; also, the signs ruled by these planets: Cancer, Sagittarius, Pisces, Taurus, and Libra.

Prakruti—finding the basic constituency in the natal chart: Looking at the planets occupying the rising sign, and the signs occupied by the Moon and the Sun, gives more specific clues as to your Ayurvedic body type. For example, a person with Aries rising, or the Moon or Sun in Aries, will have pitta or fiery tendencies. Also, if Mars is located in the first house or with the Moon or Sun, you get a similar disposition.

Vikruti—finding the temporary constituency in the dasas and gochara: Planets transiting the Lagna, Moon, or Sun will modify the body type temporarily. The current dasa will further influence the body's constitution. If a person is in Mars dasa, or if Mars is transiting over the Lagna or Moon or Sun, then the person will be more pitta (fiery) during that time. This understanding helps us know why an Ayurvedic physician can give us a different dosha reading when we get a pulse diagnosis or other Ayurvedic analysis. In general, the planets associated with the Lagna give the most information on body type.

ASTROLOGICAL ANALYSIS TIPS FOR AYURVEDA

As a general rule, the sixth house is called the *Roga Bhava,* or the "house of disease," most specifically acute or short-term diseases. The sign representing the sixth house in a specific chart will give significant clues as to the types of disease that person may be vulnerable to. You will also be able to read health significations from the planets that occupy that sixth house, its ruler and location, and those planets that have a significant aspect on the sixth. This sixth sign/house will show the dosha that will be the primary culprit in disease. For example, if Saturn is in the sixth house in Capricorn, the person will have a tendency toward vata disorders.

The eighth house also contributes to long-term diseases in a similar fashion. In addition to examining the sixth and eighth houses, a Vedic astrologer and/or Ayurvedic vaidya must look at the whole chart, noting any additional information that comes from the ascendant and any specific sign that is highly afflicted. Again, diseases tend to spring up in the dasa/bhukti periods of these planets, as well as under specific transits of these disease-inflicting planets. With the advance warning of Vedic astrology, a person can take the correct Ayurvedic preventive health measures to ward off a disease or create a state where the disease will be of less impact and duration.

If the Lagna and its ruler are weak or unfavorable, as well as the Moon and the Sun, the person's overall bala or strength might be low—and correspondingly they might have low resistance to disease.

VASTU: THE SCIENCE OF SPACE

India's *Vastu Shastra* deals with the design and construction of living and working spaces that are in harmony with the environment. The tuning mechanisms employed by Vastu are related to the flow of solar energy and polar-magnetic forces, along with Vedic astrology principles associated with the timing of construction events. Many of the doctrines of Vedic philosophy that were discussed earlier in this book are also incorporated in Vastu. For example, Vastu integrates the five elements, and places a great emphasis on eight directional forces, as marked by the compass points.

Vastu's role as a Vedic system is to provide the knowledge needed to build structures that are synchronized with the underlying life force called *prana*. This is somewhat similar to the Chinese concept of Chi and the Japanese theory of Ki. Some researchers

Vastu Purusha Mandala—Space is depicted as a human form.

feel that Feng Shui is derived from Vastu, hinted at by the original development of Buddhism from an Indian base. Vastu differs from Chinese systems of placement in that it offers its own set of directions and principles related to the placement of people and objects within space.

Vastu also incorporates a special mathematical and symbolic diagram call the *Vastu Purusha Mandala.* In Vedic design, the Earth's surface is shown as a square. This square represents the four corners of the Earth and is represented as a mandala or form occupied by Purusha, the Cosmic Man. This Vastu Purusha Mandala references those locations in a building or plot of land that are beneficial for specific functions. It also indicates which part of a building generates specific strengths or weaknesses for an individual or group.

This Vastu diagram follows the Vedic convention of showing the macrocosm integrated with the microcosm. There's a specific energy in each direction of the diagram represented by the powers of a deity. If you do activities related to the characteristics of the deity, you'll be personally empowered as well as protected. The diagram below represents the deities of the *ashtadika,* or eight directions, along with their corresponding effects on humans.

A LAYOUT OF VASTU PLACEMENTS

Northwest　　　　　Moon Vayu, Lord of Wind	**North**　　　　　Mercury Kubera, Lord of Wealth	**Northeast**　　　　　Jupiter Eashana (Ishana), Supreme Lord
For Homes: Guests, storage, maids, garage, pets and other animals, toilet, second choice for kitchen	*For Homes:* Storage of valuables, mirrors on north wall, children's rooms (with heads west for sleep; face east to study), living room, basement	*For Homes:* Prayer/Puja room, religious shrine, open porch, living room, no toilets, no staircases, okay for basement
For Businesses: Employee lounge, storage, toilets, products sell faster when stored/presented in this area	*For Businesses:* Safe, storage of valuables	*For Businesses:* Meeting rooms, money handlers, accountants, cash register, no heavy items here, final release of product
West　　　　　Saturn Varuna, Lord of Waters	**Center/Brahma Sthana** Akasha or undifferentiated space Brahma, Lord of Creation	**East**　　　　　Sun Surya, Lord of Health; or Indra, Chief of the Gods
For Homes: Children's rooms (with heads west to sleep; face east to study), study area, dining room	*For Homes:* Silent area with no human activity, courtyard, area for religious shrines	*For Homes:* Bath, dining room, storage of liquids (ghee, oil, milk, etc.), washroom, children's rooms, living room, family room, big windows, basement, mirrors on east wall
For Businesses: Build products here	*For Businesses:* No business activity, shrine for business	*For Businesses:* Storage of liquids
Southwest　　　　　Rahu Nirriti, Goddess of Dissolution, some say of the Earth or Bhoomi	**South**　　　　　Mars Yama, Lord of Death	**Southeast**　　　　　Venus Agni, Lord of Fire
For Homes: Master bedroom, storage of valuables, heavy items, no pujas in bedrooms, no toilets	*For Homes:* Dining room, bedroom, no main entrances	*For Homes:* Kitchen (face east to cook), fireplace, major electrical appliances, computers, garage (best if separate from house), weapons, exercise area, toilet (if not in NW), no bedrooms
For Business: Administrators, owners, business planning and development	*For Business:* No main entrances	*For Business:* Electrical equipment, furnaces, stoves, computers, power plants

A Comment in Closing . . .

This marks the end of the book. In many different ways, we have explored how Vedic astrology is the Science of Time. It tells us about our karma and how to behave over time in a way that helps us become healthier and happier—with ourselves and in relationship to others. Vedic astrology helps us understand our action in all phases of life: health, relationships, wealth, career, and just about everything, since it casts its light on all of life. Vedic astrology looks at our life in terms of the past, present, and future, enabling us to protect ourselves against potential dangers and to maximize our success with upcoming opportunities.

Hopefully you've enjoyed the principles and practices of Vedic astrology represented in this book. Some of these principles are easier to grasp initially, while others will require repeating before they sink in fully. Just enjoy your studies, and don't try too hard to understand it all at once. The knowledge will find a place to stay in your being. The information in this small book can help you in your own studies or make you more aware of the possibilities when you go for a consultation with an experienced Vedic astrologer. May your future be a sunny place!

Finally, you'll find some helpful supplemental material in the Appendix that follows, and of course a nice CD-ROM containing the Starter Edition of Parashara's Light Software by GeoVision and a few additional features we've slipped in.

This world is considered an ocean of bliss where every action is deemed a wave of joy.

RUNNING THE ENCLOSED FREE
VEDIC ASTROLOGY CD FROM GEOVISION

The enclosed CD contains a "Starter's Edition" of Parashara's Light software. This SE version has been created to give you an overview of this fine Vedic astrology program and provides a limited set of functions that you can run from the CD without the need of installation. This Starter's Edition of Parashara's Light software allows you to calculate your Vedic astrology chart. It also tells you what the various chart elements mean in order to help you read the chart properly. Used along with this book, it will allow you to create your own example charts to study from— a great boon for learners.

TO RUN THE CD, FOLLOW THESE STEPS:

• Insert the disc in the CD drive of your computer. An opening screen should appear automatically. If no opening screen appears, click on the Start menu, select Run, and type in d:\setup.exe. Click OK. (If your CD has a different drive letter assigned, substitute "d:\ " for the correct letter.)

- Click on "Run Parashara's Light SE Version" to launch the program.

If you wish to purchase a full version of this software, you can place your order with GeoVision sales. Visit their Website: **www.parashara.com**.

If you're still having difficulty with running the software, you can visit **www. parashara.com/vasp.htm** and look for the "Vedic Astrology Simply Put FAQ" section for more information.

Please do not contact the author or the publisher regarding technical problems. This software is being provided as starter edition freeware, and as such does not provide free technical support. While it has been tested on current PC platforms, the software on the enclosed CD-ROM is provided "as is" and cannot be guaranteed to run on future operating systems.

VEDIC RESOURCES

VEDIC ASTROLOGY SOFTWARE

Parashara's Light
Geovision Software, Inc.
P.O. Box 2152
Fairfield, IA 52556
800-459-6847
www.parashara.com

JYOTISH GEM DEALERS

Jay Boyle Design
P.O. Box 2333
Fairfield, IA 52556
800-559-5090
www.astrologicalgem.com

Healing Gems
P.O. Box 86927
Phoenix, AZ 85080
800-552-1321
www.healinggems.com

Hanumant Gems and Handicrafts
Nagar, Muni-Ki-Reti
Near Taxi Stand
Pin 249192,
Rishikesh (India)
Tel: 91-135-2434334,
www.gemsandhandicrafts.com

Sheela Jewelers
18505 Pioneer Blvd.
Artesia, CA 90701
562-809-0227

Vinacour Gems
Leon Weiner
3460 Marron Rd. Ste. 103-360
Oceanside, CA 92056
760-758-1434

Art of Legend India
(Handicrafts Division)
Sandeep Jain
Tel: 91-7422-253200
www.artoflegendindia.com

MAGAZINES

Hinduism Today
Himalayan Academy
Publishers
107 Kaholalele Rd.
Kapaa, HI 96746-9304
800-890-1008
www.hinduismtoday.com

The Astrological Magazine
Raman Publications
Nehru Circle, Seshadripuram
Bangalore, India 560 020
Tel: 91-80-33486
www.astrologicalmagazine.com

VEDIC EDUCATION

American College of Vedic Astrology (ACVA)
P.O. Box 2149
Sedona, AZ 86339
928-282-6595
www.vedicastrology.org

British Association for Vedic Astrology (BAVA)
74 Saxon Way
Romsey, Hampshire
SO51 5RH England
www.bava.org

Council of Vedic Astrology
www.councilvedicastrology.org

MEDITATION EDUCATION

The Transcendental Meditation Program™
The official TM site
www.tm.org

AYURVEDA CLINICS

Maharishi Ayurveda
The official site for Maharishi Ayurvedic Products International (MAPI)
www.mapi.com/en/pages/ayurveda.html

Kauai Center for Holistic Medicine
Dr. Suhas Kshirsagar, BAMS, MD, is a classically trained Ayurvedic physician
www.hawaiiholisticmedicine.com/dr_suhas_kshirsagar.php

VEDIC TEMPLES

San Marga Iraivan Temple
The Iraivan Temple at Kauai's Hindu Monastery
107 Kaholalele Rd.
Kapaa, HI 96746-9304
800-890-1008
www.himalayanacademy.com/ssc/hawaii/iraivan/

Temples and Ashrams World Wide
www.garamchai.com/temples.htm

VEDIC ASTROLOGY CONSULTATIONS

You can contact the author at wlevacy@vedicastrologer.com and visit his Website:
www.vedicastrologer.com

❈ ❈ ❈ ❈ ❈

Bibliography

Ayurvedic Astrology, Dr. David Frawley, Twin Lakes, WI: Lotus Press, 2005

Beneath a Vedic Sky: An Introduction to the Astrology of Ancient India, William R. Levacy, Carlsbad, CA: Hay House, 1999

Beneath a Vedic Sun: Discover Your Life Purpose with Vedic Astrology, William R. Levacy, Carlsbad, CA: Hay House, 2006

(Varahamihira's) Brihat Jataka, B.S. Rao, Bangalore: Moltilal Banarsidas, 1986

Brihat Parasara Hora, Maharishi Parasara, Bombay: Chowkhamba, 1963

Brihat Parasara Hora Sastra, Maharishi Parasara, New Delhi: Sagar Publications, 1994

Handbook of Vastu, B. Niranjan Babu, New Delhi: UBS Publisher's Dist. Ltd., 1997

Hora-sara, Prithuyasas, son of Varahmihira, New Delhi: Ranjan Publications, 1982

How to Judge a Horoscope, B.V. Raman, Delhi: Motilal Banarsidass Publishers, 1991

Light on Life: An Introduction to the Astrology of India, Hart de Fouw, Twin Lakes, WI: Lotus Press, 2003

Muhurtha, B. V. Raman, Bangalore: IBH Prakashana, 1979

The Nakshatras:The Lunar Mansions of Vedic Astrology, Dennis Harness, Ph.D., Twin Lakes, WI: Lotus Press, 1999

Perfect Health, Deepak Chopra, M.D., New York: Harmony Books, 1991

A Thousand Suns: Designing Your Future with Vedic Astrology, Linda Johnsen, Saint Paul, MN: Yes International Publishers, 2004

Vedic Astrology, Komilla Sutton, London: Chrysalis Books, 2000

Vedic Astrology: A Guide to the Fundamentals of Jyotish, Ronnie Gale Dreyer, Delhi: New Age Books, 2005

What's Your Dosha, Baby? Lisa Marie Coffey, New York: Marlowe & Company, 2004

Acknowledgments

Special thanks go out in this book to my dear Peggy for all her support and love. Thanks to Margie Corman, as well, for her assistance. I want to also give credit to the accomplished artists and their managers who contributed so much to this book: Arumugan Manivelu, Naresh Malhotra, Tulasiram Laliwal, and Bhupendra Bairagi. Thanks to Tim Jones, Deepak Ganeriwala, Yupa Kiratiyannond, Rajesh Madhyestha, Sandeep Jain, and Dean and Patricia Draznin.

I would also like to thank Bangalore (Suresh) Sureshwara and his wife, Sumathi, for coordinating paintings from Chennai and for introducing me to Manivelu. Gayatri Devi Vasudev gave me some good tips on finding artists in India. Marci Shimoff picked up some fine art for me during one of her trips to India.

Niranjan Babu has always been a great source of my Vastu knowledge, and Dr. Suhas was inspirational. I also want to note the generosity of the monks at the Kauai monastery for allowing me to use some of the art from their magazine, *Hinduism Today*. Thanks to Ceyonswami and Palaniswami.

I finally want to thank the folks at Hay House, especially Jill Kramer and Christy Salinas, who were so patient in allowing me the extra time it took to coordinate all the international dealings needed to obtain the wonderful artwork for this book.

❈ ❈ ❈ ❈ ❈

About the Author

William R. Levacy, the author of *Beneath a Vedic Sky* and *Beneath a Vedic Sun,* holds a B.A. in literature and an M.A. in education, and has been a practitioner of Vedic astrology, or *Jyotish,* as it's called in India, since 1983. He received a master's degree in the Science of Creative Intelligence in 1977 from Maharishi European Research University, where he concentrated his studies on Vedic science. In 1996, Bill was one of a very few Westerners to receive the prestigious Jyotish Kovid award from the Indian Council of Astrological Sciences (ICAS). He has also been instrumental in developing curriculum for the American College of Vedic Astrology. His two decades of experience as a business consultant in the aerospace industry contribute to the practical yet personal nature of his readings. Bill resides in Southern California.

Website: **www.vedicastrologer.com**

We hope you enjoyed this Hay House book. If you'd like to receive a free catalog featuring additional Hay House books and products, or if you'd like information about the Hay Foundation, please contact:

Hay House, Inc.
P.O. Box 5100
Carlsbad, CA 92018-5100

(760) 431-7695 or **(800) 654-5126**
(760) 431-6948 (fax) or **(800) 650-5115 (fax)**
www.hayhouse.com® • **www.hayfoundation.org**

Published and distributed in Australia by:
Hay House Australia Pty. Ltd. • 18/36 Ralph St. • Alexandria NSW 2015 • *Phone:* 612-9669-4299 • *Fax:* 612-9669-4144
www.hayhouse.com.au

Published and distributed in the United Kingdom by:
Hay House UK, Ltd. • 292B Kensal Rd., London W10 5BE • *Phone:* 44-20-8962-1230 • *Fax:* 44-20-8962-1239 • www.hayhouse.co.uk

Published and distributed in the Republic of South Africa by:
Hay House SA (Pty), Ltd., P.O. Box 990, Witkoppen 2068 • *Phone/Fax:* 27-11-706-6612 • orders@psdprom.co.za

Published in India by: Hay House Publications (India) Pvt. Ltd.,
Muskaan Complex, Plot No. 3, B-2, Vasant Kunj, New Delhi 110 070 • *Phone:* 91-11-4176-1620 • *Fax:* 91-11-4176-1630
www.hayhouseindia.co.in

Distributed in Canada by: Raincoast
9050 Shaughnessy St., Vancouver, B.C. V6P 6E5 • *Phone:* (604) 323-7100 • *Fax:* (604) 323-2600 • www.raincoast.com

Tune in to **HayHouseRadio.com**® for the best in inspirational talk radio featuring top
Hay House authors! And, sign up via the Hay House USA Website to receive the Hay House
online newsletter and stay informed about what's going on with your favorite authors. You'll
receive bimonthly announcements about Discounts and Offers, Special Events, Product Highlights,
Free Excerpts, Giveaways, and more!
www.hayhouse.com®